Selections from the

World's Devotional Classics

Volume V I

Taylor to Patrick

Jeremy Taylor

Selections
from the
World's
Devotional
Classics

EDITED BY
Robert Scott and George W. Gilmore
Editors of The Homiletic Review

———

IN TEN VOLUMES

Volume VI
Taylor to Patrick

FUNK & WAGNALLS COMPANY
NEW YORK AND LONDON

242
S428s
v.6

Contents Volume Six

Selections

Prayers

SELECTIONS FROM

The Rule and Exercises of Holy Living

BY

JEREMY TAYLOR

JEREMY TAYLOR

The son of a barber, became an English bishop, theologian, and devotional writer; born at Cambridge August 15, 1613; died at Lisburn, Ireland, August 13, 1667. He studied at Gonville and Caius College, Cambridge (B. A., 1630-31; M. A., 1633-34; D.D., Oxford, 1642). He attracted the attention of Archbishop Laud, who procured for him a fellowship, 1636, at All Soul's, Oxford, and made him his chaplain. He was also made chaplain to the king. In 1638 he became rector of Uppingham, and in 1643 rector of Overstone, Northamptonshire. Taylor was three times in prison. In 1644 he was a prisoner with the army of the Commonwealth; made a prisoner in Chepstow in 1654 and again in 1655. In 1645 he became one of the principals in a school at Newton Hall, Carmarthenshire, also chaplain to Richard Vaughan, earl of Carbery. In 1657-58 he ministered to a small body of Episcopalians in London. On the restoration of episcopacy he was raised in 1660-61 to the bishopric of Down and Connor, to which Dromore was afterward added. His best known works are: "Discourse of the Liberty of Prophesying" (1646); "Great Exemplar ... Life and Death of ... Jesus Christ" (1649); "Rule and Exercises of Holy Living" (1650); "Rule and Exercises of Holy Dying" (1651); "Holy Communicant" (1660); "Discourse on Baptism" (1652); "The Real Presence and Spirituall of Christ in the Blessed Sacrament Proved ... against Transubstantiation" (1654), and "Polemical and Moral Discourses" (1657).

I
Care of Our Time

He that is choice of his time will also be choice of his company, and choice of his actions, lest the first engage him in vanity and loss, and the latter, by being criminal, be a throwing his time and himself away and a going back in the accounts of eternity.

God hath given to man a short time here upon earth, and yet upon this short time eternity depends: but so, that for every hour of our life (after we are persons capable of laws, and know good from evil) we must give account to the great Judge of men and angels. And this is it which our blessed Savior told us, that we must give account for every idle word; not meaning that every word which is not destined to edification, or is less prudent, shall be reckoned for a sin; but that the time which we spend in our idle talking and unprofitable discoursings, that time which might and ought to have been employed to spiritual and useful purposes, that is to be accounted for.

For we must remember that we have a great work to do, many enemies to conquer, many evils to prevent, much danger to run through, many difficulties to be mastered, many necessities to serve, and much good to do, many children to provide for, or many friends to support, or many poor to relieve, or many diseases to cure, besides the needs of nature and of relation, our private and our public cares, and duties of the world, which necessity and the providence of God hath adopted into the family of religion.

And that we need not fear this instrument to be a snare to us, or that the duty must end in scruple, vexation, and eternal fears, we must remember that the life of every man may be so ordered (and indeed must) that it may be a perpetual serving of God. The greatest trouble and most busy trade and worldly encumbrances, when they are necessary or charitable, or profitable in order to any of those ends which we are bound to serve, whether public or private, being a doing of God's work. For God provides the good things of the world to serve the needs of nature by the labors of the plowman, the skill and pains of the artizan, and the dangers and traffic of the merchant; these men are in their callings the ministers of the divine providence, and the stewards of the creation, and servants of a great family of God, the world, in the employment of procuring necessaries for food and clothing, ornament and physic. In their pro-

4

portions also, a king and a priest and a prophet, a judge, and an advocate, doing the works of their employment according to their proper rules, are doing the work of God, because they serve those necessities which God hath made, and yet hath made no provisions for them but by their ministry. So that no man can complain that his calling takes him off from religion; his calling itself and his very worldly employment in honest trades and offices is a serving of God, and if it be moderately pursued, and according to the rules of Christian prudence, will leave void spaces enough for prayers and retirements of a more spiritual religion.

God hath given every man work enough to do, that there shall be no room for idleness; and yet hath so ordered the world that there shall be space for devotion. He that hath the fewest businesses of the world is called upon to spend more time in the dressing of his soul; and he that hath the most affairs may so order them that they shall be a service of God, whilst at certain periods they are blest with prayers and actions of religion, and all day long are hallowed by a holy intention.

However, so long as idleness is quite shut out from our lives, all the sins of wantonness, softness, and effeminacy are prevented, and there is but little room left for temptation;

and therefore to a busy man temptation is fain to climb up together with his business, and sins creep upon him only by accidents and occasions; whereas to an idle person they come in a full body, and with open violence, and the impudence of a restless importunity.

Idleness is called the sin of Sodom and her daughters (Ezek. 16:49), and indeed is the burial of a living man (Seneca), an idle person being so useless to any puposes of God and man that he is like one that is dead, unconcerned in the changes and necessities of the world; and he lives only to spend his time and eat the fruits of the earth; like a vermin or a wolf, when their time comes they die and perish, and in the meantime do no good; they neither plow nor carry burdens, all that they do is either unprofitable or mischievous.

Idleness is the greatest prodigality in the world: it throws away that which is invaluable in respect of its present use, and irreparable when it is past, being to be recovered by no power of art or nature. But the way to secure and improve our time we may practise in the following rules.

RULES FOR EMPLOYING OUR TIME: 1. In the morning, when you awake, accustom yourself to think first upon God, or something in order to his service; and at night, also, let him close thine eyes, and let your sleep be necessary and healthful, not idle and expensive of time beyond the needs and conveniences of nature; and sometimes be curious to see the preparation which the sun makes when he is coming forth from his chambers of the east.

2. Let every man that hath a calling, be diligent in pursuance of his employment, so as not lightly or without reasonable occasion to neglect it in any of those times which are usually, and by the custom of prudent persons and good husbands, employed in it.

3. Let all the intervals or void spaces of time be employed in prayers, reading, meditating works of nature, recreation, charity, friendliness and neighborhood (neighborliness), and means of spiritual and corporal health: ever remembering so to work in our calling as not to neglect the work of our "high calling," but to begin and end the day with God, with such forms of devotion as shall be proper to our necessities.

4. The resting day of Christians and festivals of the Church must in no sense be days of idleness, for it is better to plow upon holy days than to do nothing or to do viciously; but let them be spent in the works of the day, that is, of religion and charity, according to the rules appointed.

5. Avoid the company of drunkards and busybodies, and all such as are apt to talk

much to little purpose; for no man can be provident of his time that is not prudent in the choice of his company; and if one of the speakers be vain, tedious, and trifling, he that hears and he that answers in the discourse are equal losers of their time.

6. Never talk with any man or undertake any trifling employment merely to pass the time away; for every day well spent may become a day of salvation, and time rightly employed is an acceptable time. And remember that the time thou triflest away was given thee to repent in, to pray for pardon of sins, to work out thy salvation, to do the work of grace, to lay up against the day of judgment a treasure of good works, that thy time may be crowned with eternity.

7. In the midst of the works of thy calling, often retire to God in short prayers and ejaculations, and those may make up the want of those larger portions of time which it may be thou desirest for devotion, and in which thou thinkest other persons have advantage of thee; for so thou reconcilest the outward work and thy inward calling, the Church and the commonwealth, the employment of the body and the interest of thy soul! for be sure that God is present at thy breathings and hearty sighings of prayer as soon as at the longest offices of less busied persons; and thy

time is as truly sanctified by a trade and devout tho shorter prayers, as by the longer offices of those whose time is not filled up with labor and useful business.

8. Let your employment be such as may become a reasonable person, and not be a business fit for children or distracted people, but fit for your age and understanding. For a man may be very idly busy, and take great pains to so little purpose that in his labors and expense of time he shall serve no end but of folly and vanity. There are some trades that wholly serve the ends of idle persons and fools, and such as are fit to be seized upon by the severity of laws and banished from under the sun; and there are some people who are busy, but it is as Domitian was, in catching flies.

9. Let your employment be fitted to your person and calling. Some there are that employ their time in affairs infinitely below the dignity of their person, and being called by God or by the republic to help to bear great burdens and to judge a people, enfeeble their understandings and disable their persons by sordid and brutish business. Thus Nero went up and down Greece, and challenged the fiddlers at their trade; Aeropus, a Macedonian king, made lanterns; Harcatius, the king of Parthia, was a mole-catcher; and Biantes, the

Lydian, filed needles. He that is appointed to minister in holy things must not suffer secular affairs and sordid arts to eat up great portions of his employment: a clergyman must not keep a tavern, nor a judge be an inn-keeper; and it was a great idleness in Theophylact, the Patriarch, to spend his time in his stable of horses when he should have been in his study or his pulpit or saying his holy offices. Such employments are the diseases of labor, and rust of time, which it contracts not by laying still but by dirty employment.

10. Let your employment be such as becomes a Christian, that is, in no sense mingled with sin: for he that takes pains to serve the ends of covetousness, or ministers to another's lust, or keeps a shop of impurities or intemperance, is idle in the worst sense; for every hour so spent runs him backward, and must be spent again in the remaining and shorter part of his life, and spent better.

11. Persons of great quality and of no trade are to be most prudent and curious in their employment and traffic of time. They are miserable if their education hath been so loose and undisciplined as to leave them unfurnished of skill to spend their time; but most miserable are they if such misgovernment and unskilfulness make them fall into vicious and baser company, and drive on their

time by the sad minutes and periods of sin
and death. They that are learned know the
worth of time and the manner how well to
improve a day; and they are to prepare themselves for such purposes in which they may be
most useful in order to arts or arms, to counsel
in public or government in their country: but
for others of them that are unlearned let them
choose good company, such as may not tempt
them to a vice or join with them in any, but
that may supply their defects by counsel and
discourse by way of conduct and conversation.
Let them learn easy and useful things, read
history and the laws of the land, learn the
customs of their country, the condition of
their own estate, profitable and charitable con-
trivances of it; let them study prudently to
govern their families, learn the burdens of
their tenants, the necessities of their neighbors, and in their proportions supply them,
and reconcile their enmities, and prevent their
lawsuits, or quickly end them; and in this
glut of leisure and disemployment, let them
set apart greater portions of their time for
religion, and the necessities of their souls.

12. Let the women of noble birth and great
fortunes do the same things in their proportions and capacities—nurse their children,
look to the affairs of the house, visit poor
cottages and relieve their necessities, be cour-

teous to the neighborhood, learn in silence of their husbands or their spiritual guides, read good books, pray often, and speak little, and learn to do good works for necessary uses; for by that phrase St. Paul expresses the obligation of Christian women to good housewifery and charitable provisions for their family and neighborhood.

13. Let all persons of all conditions avoid all delicacy and niceness in their clothing or diet, because such softness engages them upon great misspendings of their time, while they dress and comb out all their opportunities of their morning devotion and half the day's severity, and sleep out the cares and provision for their souls.

14. Let every one of every condition avoid curiosity and all inquiry into things that concern them not. For all business in things that concern us not is an employing our time to no good of ours, and therefore not in order to a happy eternity. In this account our neighbor's necessities are not to be reckoned; for they concern us as one member is concerned in the grief of another; but going from house to house tattlers and busybodies, which are the canker and rust of idleness as idleness is the rust of time, are reproved by the apostle in severe language, and forbidden in order to this exercise.

15. As much as may be, cut off all impertinent and useless employment of your life, unnecessary and phantastic visits, long waitings upon great personages, where neither duty, nor necessity, nor charity, obliges us; all vain meetings, all laborious trifles, and whatsoever spends much time to no real, civil, religious, or charitable purpose.

16. Let not your recreations be lavish spenders of your time, but choose such which are healthful, short, transient, recreative, and apt to refresh you; but at no hand dwell upon them or make them your great employment, for he that spends his time in sports, and calls it recreation, is like him whose garment is all made of fringes, and his meat nothing but sauces; they are healthless, chargeable, and useless. And therefore avoid such games which require much time or long attendance, or which are apt to steal thy affections from more severe employments. For to whatsoever thou hast given thy affections thou wilt not grudge to give thy time. Natural necessity and the example of St. John (who recreated himself with sporting with a tame partridge) teach us that it is lawful to relax and unbend our bow, but not to suffer it to be unready or unstrung.

17. Set apart some portions of every day for more solemn devotion and religious em-

ployment, which be severe in observing; and if variety of employment, or prudent affairs, or civil society press upon you, yet so order thy rule that the necessary parts of it be not omitted; and tho just occasions may make our prayers shorter, yet let nothing but a violent, sudden, and impatient necessity make thee upon any one day wholly to omit thy morning and evening devotions; which if you be forced to make very short, you may supply and lengthen with ejaculations and short retirements in the daytime in the midst of your employment or of your company.

18. Do not the work of God negligently and idly (Jer. 47:10); let not thy heart be upon the world, when thy hand is lift up in prayer: and be sure to prefer an action of religion in its place and proper season before all worldly pleasure, letting secular things (that may be dispensed within themselves) in these circumstances wait upon the other; not like the patriarch who ran from the altar of St. Sophia to his stable in his pontificals, and in the midst of his office, to see a colt newly fallen from his beloved and much valued mare Phorante. More prudent and severe was that of Sir Thomas More, who being sent for by the king when he was at his prayers in public, returned answer, he would attend him when he had first performed his

service to the King of Kings. And it did
honor to Rusticus that when letters from
Cæsar were given to him, he refused to open
them till the philosopher had done his lecture.
In honoring God and doing his work put forth
all thy strength; for of that time only thou
mayest be most confident that it is gained
which is prudently and zealously spent in
God's service.

19. When the clock strikes, or however else
you shall measure the day, it is good to say a
short ejaculation every hour, that the parts
and returns of devotion may be the measure
of your time; and do so also in all the breaches
of thy sleep, that those spaces which have in
them no direct business of the world may be
filled with religion.

20. If by thus doing you have not secured
your time by an early and forehanded care,
yet be sure by a timely diligence to redeem
the time, that is, to be pious and religious in
such instances in which formerly you have
sinned, and to bestow your time especially
upon such graces, the contrary whereof you
have formerly practised, doing actions of
chastity and temperance with as great a zeal
and earnestness as you did once act your
uncleanness; and then by all arts to watch
against your present and future dangers, from
day to day securing your standing: this is

properly to redeem your time, that is, to buy your security of it at the rate of any labor and honest arts.

21. Let him that is most busied set apart some time every year in which, for the time quitting all worldly business, he may attend wholly to fasting and prayer (1 Cor. 7:5), and the dressing of his soul by confessions, meditations, and attendance upon God; that he may make up his accounts, renew his vows, make amends for his carelessness, and retire back again from whence levity and the vanities of the world, or the opportunities of temptations, or the distraction of secular affairs have carried him.

22. In this we shall be much assisted, and we shall find the work more easy, if before we sleep every night we examine the actions of the past day with a particular scrutiny, if there have been any accidents extraordinary; as long discourse, a feast, much business, variety of company. If nothing but common hath happened, the less examination will suffice; only let us take care that we sleep not without such a recollection of the action of the day as may represent anything that is remarkable and great either to be the matter of sorrow or thanksgiving: for other things a general care is proportionable.

23. Let all these things be done prudently

and moderately, not with scruple and vexation. For these are good advantages, but the particulars are not divine commandments, and therefore are to be used as shall be found expedient to every one's condition. For, provided that our duty be secured, for the degrees and for the instrument every man is permitted to himself and the conduct of such who shall be appointed to him. He is happy that can secure every hour to a sober or a pious employment; but the duty consists not scrupulously in minutes or half-hours, but in greater portions of time; provided that no minute be employed in sin, and the great portions of our time be spent in sober employment, and all the appointed days and some portions of every day be allowed for religion. In all the lesser parts of time we are left to our own elections and prudent management, and to the consideration of the great degrees and differences of glory that are laid up in heaven for us, according to the degrees of our care and piety and diligence.

THE BENEFITS OF THIS EXERCISE: This exercise, besides it hath influence upon our whole lives, it hath a special efficacy for the preventing of (1) beggarly sins, that is those sins which idleness and beggary usually betray men to; such as are lying, flattery, stealing, and dissimulation. (2) It is a proper antidote against carnal sins, and such as proceed from fulness of bread and emptiness of employment. (3) It is a great instrument of preventing the smallest sins and irregularities of our life; which usually creep upon idle, disemployed, and curious persons. (4) It not only teaches us to avoid evil, but engages us upon doing good as the proper business of all our days. (5) It prepares us so against sudden changes, that we shall not easily be surprized at the sudden coming of the day of the Lord; for he that is curious of his time, will not easily be unready and unfurnished.

II

Purity of Intention

That we should intend and design God's glory in every action we do, whether it be natural or chosen, is exprest by St. Paul, "Whether ye eat or drink, do all to the glory of God" (1 Cor. 10:31). Which rule when we observe, every action of nature becomes religious, and every meal is an act of worship, and shall have its reward in its proportion as well as an act of prayer. Blessed be that goodness and grace of God which, out of infinite desire to gratify and save mankind, would make the very works of nature capable of becoming acts of virtue, that all our lifetime we may do him service.

This grace is so excellent, that it sanctifies the most common actions of our lives; and yet so necessary, that without it the very best actions of our devotion are imperfect and vicious. For he that prays out of custom, or gives alms for praise, or fasts to be accounted religious, is but a Pharisee in his devotion, and a beggar in his alms, and an hypocrite in his fast. But a holy end sanctifies all these and all other actions which can be made holy, and gives distinctions to them, and procures acceptance.

For, as to know the end distinguishes a man from a beast, so to choose a good end distinguishes him from an evil man. Hezekiah repeated his good deeds upon his sick-bed, and obtained favor of God; but the Pharisee was accounted insolent for doing the same thing, because this man did it to upbraid his brother, the other to obtain a mercy of God. Zacharias questioned with the angel about his message, and was made speechless for his incredulity; but the blessed Virgin Mary questioned too, and was blameless; for she did it to inquire after the manner of the thing, but he did not believe the thing itself: he doubted of God's power, or the truth of the messenger; but she only of her own incapacity. This was it which distinguished the mourning of David from the exclamation of Saul, the confession of Pharaoh from that of Manasses, the tears of Peter from the repentance of Judas: "For the praise is not in the deed done, but in the manner of its doing. If a man visits his sick friend and watches at his pillow for charity's sake and because of his old affection, we approve it; but if he does it in hope of legacy, he is a vulture and only watches for the carcass. The same things are honest and dishonest; the manner of doing them, and the end of the design, makes the distinction" (Seneca).

Holy intention is to the actions of a man that which the soul is to the body, or form to its matter, or the root to the tree, or the sun to the world, or the fountain to the river, or the base to a pillar; for without these the body is a dead trunk, the matter is sluggish, the tree is a block, the world is darkness, the river is quickly dry, the pillar rushes into flatness and ruin; and the action is sinful or unprofitable and vain. The poor farmer that gave a dish of cold water to Artaxerxes was rewarded with a golden goblet, and he that gives the same to a disciple in the name of a disciple shall have a crown; but if he gives water in despite when the disciple needs wine or a cordial, his reward shall be to want that water to cool his tongue.

But this duty must be reduced to rules.

RULES FOR OUR INTENTION: 1. In every action reflect upon the end; and in your undertaking it, consider why you do it, and what you propound to yourself for a reward and to your action as its end.

2. Begin every action in the name of the Father, of the Son, and of the Holy Ghost: the meaning of which is, (1) that we be careful that we do not the action without the permission or warrant of God. (2) That we design it to the glory of God, if not in the direct action yet at least in its consequence; if not in the particular yet at least in the whole order of things and accidents. (3) That it may be so blest that what you intend for innocent and holy purposes may not, by any chance or abuse or misunderstanding of men, be turned into evil or made the occasion of sin.

3. Let every action of concernment be begun with prayer, that God would not only bless the action but sanctify your purpose; and make an oblation of the action to God, holy and well intended actions being the best oblations and presents we can make to God: and when God is entitled to them, he will the rather keep the fire upon the altar bright and shining.

4. In the prosecution of the action, renew and reinkindle your purpose by short ejaculations to those purposes: "Not unto us, O Lord, not unto us, but unto thy name let all praise be given! and consider now I am working the work of God. I am his servant, I am in happy employment, I am doing my Master's business, I am not at my own disposal, I am using his talents, and all the gain must be his"; for then, be sure, as the glory is his, the reward shall be thine. If thou bringest his goods home with increase, he will make thee ruler over cities.

5. Have a care that while the altar thus sends up a holy flame, thou dost not suffer the birds to come and carry away the sacrifice: that is, let not that which began well, and was intended for God's glory, decline and end in thy own praise or temporal satisfaction or sin. A story told to represent the vileness of unchastity is well begun: but if the female auditor be pleased with thy language, and begins rather to like thy person for thy story than to dislike the crime, be watchful lest this goodly head of gold descend in silver and brass and end in the iron and clay, like Nebuchadnezzar's image; for from the end it shall have its name and reward.

6. If any accidental event which was not first intended by thee come to pass, let it not be

taken into thy purposes, not at all be made use of: as if, by telling a true story you can do an ill turn to your enemy, by no means do it; but when the temptation is found out, turn all thy enmity upon that.

7. In every more solemn action of religion, join together many good ends, that the consideration of them may entertain all your affections; and that when any one ceases, the purity of your intention may be supported by another supply. He that fasts only to tame a rebellious body, when he is provided of a remedy either in grace or nature, may be tempted to leave off his fasting. But he that in his fast intends the mortification of every unruly appetite, and to accustom himself to bear the yoke of the Lord, a contempt of the pleasures of meat and drink, humiliation of all the wilder thoughts, obedience and humility, austerity and charity, and the convenience and assistance to devotion, and to do an act of repentance, whatever happens, will have reason enough to make him to continue his purpose and to sanctify it. And certain it is, the more good ends are designed in an action, the more degrees of excellency the man obtains.

8. If any temptation to spoil your purposes happens in a religious duty, do not presently omit the action, but rather strive to

rectify your intention and to mortify the temptation. St. Bernard taught us this rule: for when the devil, observing him to preach excellently and to do much benefit to his hearers, tempted him to vainglory, hoping that the good man to avoid that would cease preaching, he gave this answer only, "I neither began for thee, neither for thee will I make an end."

9. In all actions which are of long continuance, deliberation, and abode, let your holy and pious intention be actual, that is, that it be by a special prayer or action, by a peculiar act of resignation or oblation given to God. But in smaller actions, and little things and indifferent, fail not to secure a pious habitual intention; that is, that it be included within your general care that no action have an ill end; and that it be comprehended in your general prayers, whereby you offer yourself and all you do to God's glory.

10. Call not every temporal end a defiling of thy intention; but only, (1) when it contradicts any of the ends of God; or (2) when it is principally intended in an act of religion. For sometimes a temporal end is part of our duty; and such are all the actions of our calling, whether our employment be religious or civil. We are commanded to provide for our family; but if the minister of divine offices

shall take upon him that holy calling for covetous or ambitious ends, or shall not design the glory of God principally and especially, he hath polluted his hands and his heart, and the fire of the altar is quenched, or it sends forth nothing but the smoke of mushrooms or unpleasant gums. And it is a great unworthiness to prefer the interest of a creature before the ends of God the almighty Creator.

But because many cases may happen in which a man's heart may deceive him, and he may not well know what is in his own spirit; therefore by these following signs we shall best make a judgment whether our intentions be pure and our purposes holy.

SIGNS OF PURITY OF INTENTION: 1. It is probable our hearts are right with God and our intentions innocent and pious, if we set upon actions of religion or civil life with an affection proportionate to the quality of the work; that we act our temporal affairs with a desire no greater than our necessity; and that in actions of religion we be zealous, active, and operative so far as prudence will permit; but in all cases, that we value a religious design before a temporal, when otherwise they are in equal order to their several ends; that is, that whatsoever is necessary in order to our soul's health, be higher esteemed than what is for bodily; and the necessities, the indispensable necessities of the spirit, be served before the needs of nature, when they are required in their several circumstances; or plainer yet, when we choose any temporal inconvenience rather than commit a sin, and when we choose to do a duty rather than to get gain. But he that does his recreation or his merchandise cheerfully, promptly, readily, and busily, and the works of religion slowly, flatly, and without appetite, and the spirit moves like Pharaoh's chariots when the wheels were off, it is a sign that his heart is not right with God, but it cleaves too much to the world.

2. It is likely our hearts are pure and our intentions spotless when we are not solicitous of the opinion and censures of men, but only that we do our duty, and be accepted of God. For our eyes will certainly be fixt there from whence we expect our reward: and if we desire that God should approve us, it is a sign we do his work and expect him our paymaster.

3. He that does as well in private between God and his own soul as in public, in pulpits, in theaters, and market places, hath given himself a good testimony that his purposes are full of honesty, nobleness, and integrity. For what Elkanah said to the mother of

Samuel, "Am I not better to thee than ten sons?" is most certainly most verified concerning God, that he who is to be our Judge is better than ten thousand witnesses. But he that would have his virtues published studies not virtue but glory. "He is not just that will not be just without praise: but he is a righteous man that does justice, when to do so is made infamous; and he is a wise man who is delighted with an ill name that is well gotten (Seneca, Epist. 113). And indeed that man hath a strange covetousness or folly that is not contented with this reward, that he hath pleased God (St. Gregory, Moral 8, chap. 23). And see what he gets by it. He that does good works for praise or secular ends, sells an inestimable jewel for a trifle; and that which would purchase heaven for him he parts with for the breath of the people, which at the best is but air, and that not often wholesome" (St. Chrysostom *Compun. bordis* 50 : 2).

4. It is well also when we are not solicitous or troubled concerning the effect and event of all our actions; but that being first by prayer recommended to him, is left at his disposal: for then in case the event be not answerable to our desires or to the efficacy of the instrument, we have nothing left to rest in but the honesty of our purposes, which it is

the more likely we have secured by how much more we are indifferent concerning the success. St. James converted but eight persons when he preached in Spain, and our blessed Savior converted fewer than his own disciples did: and if thy labors prove unprosperous, if thou beest much troubled at that, it is certain thou didst not think thyself secure of a reward from thine intention, which thou mightest have done if it had been pure and just.

5. He loves virtue for God's sake and its own that loves and honors it wherever it is to be seen; but he that is envious or angry at a virtue that is not his own, at the perfection or excellency of his neighbor, is not covetous of the virtue but of its reward and reputation, and then his intentions are polluted. It was a great ingenuity in Moses that wished all the people might be prophets; but if he had designed his own honor, he would have prophesied alone. But he that desireth only that the work of God and religion shall go on is pleased with it, whoever is the instrument.

6. He that despises the world and all its appendant vanities is the best judge, and the most secure of his intentions, because he is the furthest removed from a temptation. Every degree of mortification is a testimony of the

purity of our purposes: and in what degree we despise sensual pleasure, or secular honors, or worldly reputation, in the same degree we shall conclude our heart right to religion and spiritual designs.

7. When we are not solicitous concerning the instruments and means of our actions, but use those means which God hath laid before us with resignation, indifference, and thankfulness, it is a good sign that we are rather intent upon the end of God's glory than our own conveniency or temporal satisfaction. He that is indifferent whether he serve God in riches or in poverty is rather a seeker of God than of himself; and he that will throw away a good book because it is not curiously gilded is more curious to please his eye than to inform his understanding.

8. When a temporal end, consisting with a spiritual and pretended to be subordinate to it, happens to fail and be defeated, if we can rejoice in that so God's glory may be secured and the interests of religion, it is a great sign our hearts are right and our ends prudently designed and ordered.

When our intentions are thus balanced, regulated and discerned, we may consider, (1) that this exercise is of so universal efficacy in the whole course of a holy life that it is like the soul to every holy action, and must be provided for in every undertaking, and is of itself alone sufficient to make all natural and indifferent actions to be adopted into the family of religion.

(2) That there are some actions which are usually reckoned as parts of our religion, which yet of themselves are so relative and imperfect that without the purity of intention they degenerate: and unless they be directed and proceed on to those purposes which God designed them to, they return into the family of common secular and sinful actions. Thus alms are for charity, fasting for temperance, prayer is for religion, humiliation is for humility, austerity or suffering is in order to the virtue of patience: and when these actions fail of their several ends or are not directed to their own purposes, alms are misspent, fasting is an impertinent trouble, prayer is but lip-labor, humiliation is but hypocrisy, sufferance is but vexation; for such were the alms of the Pharisee, the fast of Jezebel, the prayer of Judah reproved by the Prophet Isaiah, the humiliation of Ahab, the martyrdom of heretics; in which nothing is given to God but the body or the forms of religion, but the soul and the power of godliness is wholly wanting.

(3) We are to consider that no intention can sanctify an unholy or unlawful action.

Saul the king disobeyed God's commandment, and spared the cattle of Amalek to reserve the best for sacrifice; and Saul the Pharisee persecuted the Church of God with a design to do God service: and they that killed the apostles had also good purposes, but they had unhallowed actions. When there is both truth in election and charity in the intention, when we go to God in ways of his own choosing or approving, then our eye is single, and our hands are clean, and our hearts are pure (St. Bernard, "Lib. de Precept."). But when a man does evil that good may come of it or good to an evil purpose, that man does like him that rolls himself in thorns that he may sleep easily: he roasts himself in the fire that he may quench his thirst with his own sweat; he turns his face to the east that he may go to bed with the sun. I end this with the saying of a wise heathen: "He is to be called evil, that is good only for his own sake. Regard not how full hands you bring to God, but how pure. Many cease from sin out of fear alone, not out of innocence of love of virtue" (Publius Mimus) and they (as yet) are not to be called innocent, but timorous.

III

The Practise of the Presence of God

That God is present in all places, that he sees every action, hears all discourses, and understands every thought, is no strange thing to a Christian ear, who hath been taught in this doctrine, not only by right reason and the consent of all the wise men in the world, but also by God himself in Holy Scripture. "Am I a God at hand (saith the Lord) and not a God afar off? Can any hide himself in secret places that I shall not see him? (saith the Lord). Do not I fill heaven and earth?" (Jer. 23:24). "Neither is there any creature that is not manifest in his sight: but all things are naked and open to the eyes of him with whom we have to do" (Heb. 4:13). For "in him we live and move, and have our being" (Acts 17:28). God is wholly in every place, included in no place, not bound with cords (except those of love), not divided into parts nor changeable into several shapes, filling heaven and earth with his present power, and with his never-absent nature. So St. Augustine expresses this article ("De Civit." 7:30). So that we may imagine God to be as the air and the sea, and we all enclosed in his circle, wrapt up in the lap of his infinite nature, or as infants in the wombs of their pregnant mothers: and we can no more be removed from the presence of God than from our own being.

SEVERAL MANNERS OF THE DIVINE PRESENCE: The presence of God is understood by us in several manners and to several purposes.

1. God is present by his essence, which because it is infinite can not be contained within the limits of any place: and because he is of an essential purity and spiritual nature, he can not be undervalued by being supposed present in the places of unnatural uncleanness: because as the sun reflecting upon the mud of strands and shores is unpolluted in its beams, so is God not dishonored when we suppose him in every one of his creatures, and in every part of every one of them, and is still as unmixed with any unhandsome adherence as is the soul in the bowels of the body.

2. God is everywhere present by his power. He rolls the orbs of heaven with his hand, he fixes the earth with his foot, he guides all the creatures with his eye, and refreshes them with his influence; he makes the powers of hell to shake with his terrors, and binds the devils with his word, and throws them out with his command, and sends the angels on embassies with his decrees; he hardens the

joints of infants, and confirms the bones when they are fashioned beneath secretly in the heart. He it is that assists at the numerous productions of fishes, and there is not one hollowness in the bottom of the sea but he shows himself to be Lord of it by sustaining there the creatures that come to dwell in it; and in the wilderness the bittern and the stork, the dragon and the satyr, the unicorn and the elk, live upon his provisions and revere his power and feel the force of his almightiness.

3. God is more especially present in some places by the several and more special manifestations of himself to extraordinary purposes by glory. Thus his seat is in heaven; because there he sits encircled with all the outward demonstrations of his glory, which he is pleased to show to all the inhabitants of those his inward and secret courts. And thus they that die in the Lord may be properly said to be gone to God; with whom, altho they were before, yet now they enter into his courts, into the secret of his tabernacle, into the retinue and splendor of his glory. That is called walking with God, but this is dwelling or being with him. I desire to be dissolved and to be with Christ, so said St. Paul. But this manner of the divine presence is reserved for the elect people of God, and for their portion in their country.

4. God is by grace and benediction specially present in holy places and in the solemn assemblies of his servants (Matt. 18:20; Heb. 10:25). If holy people meet in grots and dens of the earth when persecution or a public necessity disturbs the public order, circumstance, and convenience, God fails not to come thither to them; but God is also by the same or greater reason present there where they meet ordinarily by order and public authority: there God is present ordinarily, *i.e.*, at every such meeting. God will go out of his way to meet his saints when themselves are forced out of their way of order by a sad necessity; but else God's usual way is to be present in those places where his servants are appointed ordinarily to meet (Kings 5:9; Ps. 138:1, 3). But his presence there signifies nothing but a readiness to hear their prayers, to bless their persons, to accept their offices, and to like even the circumstance of orderly and public meeting. For thither prayers of consecration, the public authority separating it, and God's love of order, and the reasonable customs of religion, have in ordinary and in a certain degree fixt this manner of his presence; and he loves to have it so.

5. God is especially present in the hearts of his people by his Holy Spirit; and indeed the hearts of holy men are temples in the

truth of things, and in type and shadow they are heaven itself: for God reigns in the hearts of his servants; there is his kingdom. The power of grace hath subdued all his enemies; there is his power. They serve him night and day, and give him thanks and praise; that is his glory. This is the religion and worship of God in the temple. The temple itself is the heart of man: Christ is the High-Priest, who from thence sends up the incense of prayers, and joins them to his own intercession, and presents all together to his Father; and the Holy Ghost by his dwelling there hath also consecrated it into a temple (1 Cor. 3:16; 2 Cor. 6:16); and God dwells in our hearts by faith, and Christ by his Spirit, and the Spirit by his purities; so that we are also cabinets of the mysterious Trinity; and what is this short of heaven itself, but as infancy is short of manhood and letters of words? The same state of life it is, but not the same age. It is heaven in a looking-glass (dark, but yet true), representing the beauties of the soul, and graces of God, and the images of his eternal glory by the reality of a special presence.

6. God is especially present in the consciences of all persons, good and bad, by way of testimony and judgment; that is, he is there a Remembrancer to call our actions to mind,

a Witness to bring them to judgment, and a Judge to acquit or to condemn. And altho this manner of presence is in this life after the manner of this life, that is imperfect, and we forget many actions of our lives; yet the greatest changes of our state of grace or sin, our most considerable actions, are always present, like capital letters to an aged and dim eye: and at the day of judgment God shall draw aside the cloud, and manifest this manner of his presence more notoriously, and make it appear that he was an observer of our very thoughts, and that he only laid those things by which, because we covered with dust and negligence, were not then discerned. But when we are risen from our dust and imperfections, they all appear plain and legible.

Now the consideration of this great truth is of a very universal use in the whole course of a life of a Christian. All the consequents and effects of it are universal (St. Augustine, "De verbis dominicis," chap. 3). He that remembers that God stands a witness and a judge, beholding every secrecy, besides his impiety must have put on impudence, if he be not restrained in his temptation to sin. "For the greatest part of sin is taken away, if a man have a witness of his conversation; and he is a great despiser of God who sends a boy away when he is going to commit fornication, and yet will dare to do it, tho he knows God is present and can not be sent off: as if the eye of a little boy were more awful than the all-seeing eye of God. He is to be feared in public, he is to be feared in private: if you go forth he spies you: if you go in he sees you: when you light the candle he observes you; when you put it out, then also God marks you. Be sure that while you are in his sight, you behave yourself as becomes so holy a presence." But if you will sin, retire yourself wisely, and go where God can not see; for nowhere else can you be safe. And certainly, if men would always actually consider and really esteem this truth, that God is the great eye of the world, always watching over our actions, and an ever open ear to hear all our words, and an unwearied arm ever lifted up to crush a sinner into ruin, it would be the readiest way in the world to make sin to cease from among the children of men, and for men to approach to the blessed state of the saints in heaven, who can not sin, for they always walk in the presence and behold the face of God. This instrument is to be reduced to practise according to the following rules.

Rules of Exercising this Consideration: 1. Let this actual thought often return, that God is omnipresent, filling every place; and say with David, "Whither shall I go from thy Spirit, or whither shall I flee from thy presence? If I ascend up into heaven, thou art there: if I make my bed in hell, thou art there," etc. (Ps. 7:8). This thought by being frequent will make an habitual dread and reverence toward God, and fear in all thy actions. For it is a great necessity and engagement to do unblameably, when we act before the Judge who is infallible in his sentence, all-knowing in his information, severe in his anger, powerful in his providence, and intolerable in his wrath and indignation (Boethius, "De consol." 1:5).

2. In the beginning of actions of religion, make an act of adoration, that is, solemnly worship God, and place thyself in God's presence, and behold him with the eye of faith, and let thy desires actually fix on him as the object of thy worship, and the reason of thy hope, and the fountain of thy blessing. For when thou hast placed thyself before him, and kneelest in his presence, it is most likely all the following parts of thy devotion will be answerable to the wisdom of such an apprehension and the glory of such a presence.

3. Let everything you see represent to your spirit the presence, the excellency, and the power of God, and let your conversation with the creatures lead you unto the Creator; for

so shall your actions be done more frequently with an actual eye to God's presence, by your often seeing him in the glass of the creation. In the face of the sun you may see God's beauty; in the fire you may feel his heat warming; in the water his gentleness to refresh you: he it is that comforts your spirits when you have taken cordials, it is the dew of heaven that makes your field give you bread, and the breasts of God are the bottles that minister drink to your necessities. This philosophy, which is obvious to every man's experience, is a good advantage to our piety, and by this act of understanding our wills are checked from violence and misdemeanor.

4. In your retirement make frequent colloquies or short discoursings between God and thy own soul. "Seven times a day do I praise thee, and in the night season also I thought upon thee while I was waking." So did David: and every act of complaint or thanksgiving, every act of rejoicing or of mourning, every petition and every return of the heart in these intercourses, is a going to God, and appearing in his presence, and a representing him present to thy spirit and to thy necessity. And this was long since by a spiritual person called, "a building to God a chapel in our heart." It reconciles Martha's employment with Mary's devotion, charity and religion,

the necessities of our calling, and the employments of devotion. For thus, in the midst of the works of your trade, you may retire into your chapel (your heart) and converse with God by frequent addresses and returns.

5. Represent and offer to God acts of love and fear, which are the proper effects of this apprehension and the proper exercise of this consideration. For as God is everywhere present by his power, he calls for reverence and godly fear. As he is present to thee in all thy needs, and relieves them, he deserves thy love; and since in every action of our lives we find one or other of these apparent, and in most things we see both, it is a proper and proportionate return that, to every such demonstration of God, we express ourselves sensible of it by admiring the divine goodness, or trembling at his presence, ever obeying him because we love him, and ever obeying him because we fear to offend him. This is that which Enoch did, who thus walked with God.

6. Let us remember that God is in us, and that we are in him. We are his workmanship, let us not deface it; we are in his presence, let us not pollute it by unholy and impure actions. God hath also wrought all our works in us (Isa. 26:12); and because he rejoices in his own works, if we defile them and make them unpleasant to him, we walk perversely

with God, and he will walk crookedly toward us.

7. God is in the bowels of thy brother; refresh them when he needs it, and then you give your alms in the presence of God and to God, and he feels the relief which thou providest for thy brother.

8. God is in every place: suppose it therefore to be a church, and that decency of deportment and piety of carriage which you are taught by religion or by custom, or by civility and public manners, to use in churches, the same use in all places; with this difference only, that in churches let your deportment be religious in external forms and circumstances also; but there and everywhere let it be religious in abstaining from spiritual indecencies, and in readiness to do good actions; that it may not be said of us as God once complained of his people, "Why hath my beloved done wickedness in my house" (Jer. 6:15, Vulgate).

9. God is in every creature: be cruel toward none, neither abuse any by intemperance. Remember that the creatures and every member of thy own body is one of the lesser cabinets and receptacles of God. They are such which God hath blest with presence, hallowed by his touch, and separated from unholy use by making them belong to his dwelling.

10. He walks as in the presence of God that converses with him in frequent prayer and frequent communion, that runs to him in all his necessities, that asks counsel of him in all his doubtings, that opens all his wants to him, that weeps before him for his sins, that asks remedy and support for his weakness, that fears him as a Judge, reverences him as a Lord, obeys him as a Father. and loves him as a Patron.

THE BENEFITS OF THIS EXERCISE: The benefits of this consideration and exercise being universal upon all the parts of piety, I shall less need to specify any particulars; but yet, most properly, this exercise of considering the divine presence is:

1. An excellent help to prayer, producing in us reverence and awfulness to the divine majesty of God, and actual devotion in our offices.

2. It produces a confidence in God and fearlessness of our enemies, patience in trouble and hope of remedy, since God is so nigh in all our sad accidents, he is a disposer of the hearts of men and the events of things, he proportions out our trials and supplies us with the remedy, and where his rod strikes us, his staff supports us. To which we may add this, that God, who is always with us, is especially by promise with us in tribulation

to turn the misery into a mercy, and that our greatest trouble may become our advantage by entitling us to a new manner of the divine presence.

3. It is apt to produce joy and rejoicing in God, we being more apt to delight in the partners and witnesses of our conversation, every degree of mutual abiding and conversing being a relation and an endearment: we are of the same household with God; he is with us in our natural actions to preserve us, in our recreations to restrain us, in our public actions to applaud or reprove us, in our private to observe us, in our sleeps to watch by us, in our watchings to refresh us; if we walk with God in all his ways, as he walks with us in all ours, we shall find perpetual reasons to enable us to keep that rule of God, "Rejoice in the Lord always, and again I say rejoice." And this puts me in mind of a saying of an old religious person: "There is one way of overcoming our ghostly enemies; spiritual mirth and a perpetual bearing of God in our minds" ("Vita S. Anthoni"). This effectually resists the devil, and suffers us to receive no hurt from him.

4. This exercise is apt also to enkindle holy desires of the enjoyment of God because it produces joy, when we do enjoy him—the same desires that a weak man hath for a

defender, the sick man for a physician, the poor for a patron, the child for his father, the espoused lover for her betrothed.

5. From the same fountain are apt to issue humility of spirit, apprehensions of our great distance and our great needs or daily wants and hourly supplies, admiration of God's unspeakable mercies; it is the cause of great modesty and decency in our actions; it helps to recollection of mind and restrains the scatterings and looseness of wandering thoughts; it establishes the heart in good purposes and leadeth on to perseverance; it gains purity and perfection, according to the saying of God to Abraham, "Walk before me and be perfect," holy fear and holy love, and indeed everything that pertains to holy living; when we see ourselves placed in the eye of God, who sets us on work and will reward us plenteously. To serve him with an eye-service is very unpleasing, for he also sees the heart; and the want of this consideration was declared to be the cause why Israel sinned so grievously, "For they say, The Lord hath forsaken the earth, and the Lord seeth not: therefore the land is full of blood, and the city full of perverseness" (Ezek. 9:9; Ps. 10:11). What a child would do in the eye of his father, and a pupil before his tutor, and a wife in the presence of her husband, and a servant in the

sight of his master, let us always do the same:
for we are made a spectacle to God, to angels,
and to men; we are always in the sight and
presence of the all-seeing and almighty God,
who also is to us a Father and a Guardian, a
Husband and a Lord.

✠ ✠

Prayers and Devotions According to the Religion and Purposes of the Foregoing Considerations

I

For Grace to Spend Our Time Well

O eternal God, who from all eternity dost
behold and love thy own glories and perfections infinite, and hast created men to do the
work of God after the manner of men, and to
serve thee in this generation and according to
my capacities; give me thy grace that I may
be a curious and prudent spender of my time,
so as I may best prevent or resist all temptation and be profitable to the Christian commonwealth, and by discharging all my duty
may glorify thy name. Take from me all
slothfulness, and give me a diligent and an
active spirit and wisdom to choose my employment, that I may do works proportionable

to my person and to the dignity of a Christian, and may fill up all the spaces of my time with actions of religion and charity; that when the devil assaults me, he may not find me idle, and my dearest Lord at his sudden coming may find me busy in lawful, necessary, and pious actions, improving my talent entrusted to me by thee, my Lord, that I may enter into the joy of my Lord, to partake of his eternal felicities, even for thy mercy's sake, and for my dearest Savior's sake. AMEN.

Prayers In the Morning As Soon As We Are Drest

Humbly and reverently compose yourself, with heart lift up to God, and your head bowed, and meekly kneeling upon your knees, say the Lord's Prayer: after which use the following Collects, or as many of them as you choose.

Our Father, etc.

I

An Act of Adoration, Being the Song that the Angels Sing In Heaven

Holy, holy, holy, Lord God Almighty, which was, and is, and is to come (Rev. 11:17):

heaven and earth, angels and men, the air and the sea, give glory and honor and thanks to him that sitteth on the throne, who liveth for ever and ever (Rev. 5:10, 13). All the blessed spirits and souls of the righteous cast their crowns before the throne, and worship him that liveth for ever and ever. Thou art worthy, O Lord, to receive glory and honor and power: for thou hast created all things, and for thy pleasure they are and were created (Rev. 4:10, 11). Great and marvelous are thy works, O Lord God Almighty: just and true are thy ways, thou King of saints (Rev. 15:3). Thy wisdom is infinite, thy mercies are glorious: I am not worthy, O Lord, to appear in thy presence, before whom the angels hide their faces. O holy and eternal Jesus, Lamb of God, who wert slain from the beginning of the world, thou hast redeemed us to God by thy blood out of every nation, and hast made us unto our God kings and priests, and we shall reign with thee for ever. Blessing, honor, glory, and power, be unto him that sitteth on the throne, and to the Lamb for ever. AMEN.

II

An Act of Thanksgiving, Being the Song of David for the Morning

Sing praises unto the Lord, O ye saints of his, and give thanks to him for a remembrance of his holiness. For his wrath endureth but the twinkling of an eye, and in his pleasure is life: heaviness may endure for a night, but joy cometh in the morning. Thou, Lord, hast preserved me this night from the violence of the spirits of darkness, from all sad casualties and evil accidents, from the wrath which I have every day deserved: thou hast brought my soul out of hell; thou hast kept my life from them that go down into the pit: thou hast showed me marvelous great kindness, and hast blest me forever; the greatness of thy glory reacheth unto the heavens, and thy truth unto the clouds. Therefore shall every good man sing of thy praise without ceasing. O my God, I will give thanks to thee for ever. Hallelujah.

III

An Act of Oblation, or Presenting Ourselves to God for the Day

Most holy and eternal God, Lord and Sovereign of all the creatures, I humbly present to thy divine Majesty myself, my soul and body, my thoughts and my words, my actions and intentions, my passions and my sufferings, to be disposed by thee to thy glory, to be blest by thy providence, to be guided by thy counsel, to be sanctified by thy Spirit, and afterward that my body and soul may be received into thy glory; for nothing can perish which is under thy custody, and the enemy of souls can not devour what is thy portion nor take it out of thy hands. This day, O Lord, and all the days of my life I dedicate to thy honor, and the actions of my calling to the uses of grace, and the religion of all my days to be united to the merits and intercession of my holy Savior, Jesus, that in him and for him I may be pardoned and accepted. AMEN.

IV

An Act of Repentance or Contrition

For as for me, I am not worthy to be called thy servant, much less am I worthy to be thy son; for I am the vilest of sinners and the worst of men, a lover of the things of the world and a despiser of the things of God— proud and envious, lustful and intemperate; greedy of sin and impatient of reproof, desirous to seem holy and negligent of being so, transported with interest, fooled with presumption and false principles, disturbed with anger, with a peevish and unmortified spirit, and disordered by a whole body of sin and death. Lord pardon all my sins for my sweetest Savior's sake: thou who didst die for me, holy Jesus, save me and deliver me: reserve not my sins to be punished in the day of wrath and eternal vengeance, but wash away my sins and blot them out of thy remembrance, and purify my soul with the waters of repentance and the blood of the cross; that for what is past thy wrath may not come out against me, and for the time to come I may never provoke thee to anger, or to jealousy. O just and dear God, be pitiful and gracious to thy servant. AMEN.

V

The Prayer or Petition

Bless me, gracious God, in my calling to such purposes as thou shalt choose for me or employ me in: relieve me in my sadnesses, make my bed in my sickness, give me patience in my sorrows, confidence in thee, and grace to call upon thee in all temptations. O be thou my guide in all my actions, my protector in all dangers: give me a healthful body and a clear understanding; a sanctified and just, a charitable and humble, a religious and a contented spirit: let not my life be miserable and wretched, nor my name stained with sin and shame, nor my condition lifted up to a tempting and dangerous fortune; but let my condition be blessed, my conversation useful to my neighbors and pleasing to thee, that when my body shall lie down in its bed of darkness, my soul may pass into the regions of light and live with thee for ever, through Jesus Christ. Amen.

Evening Prayers

O eternal God, great Father of men and angels, who hast established the heavens and the earth in a wonderful order, making day and night to succeed each other; I make my humble address to thy divine majesty, begging of thee mercy and protection this night and ever. O Lord, pardon all my sins, my light and rash words, the vanity and impiety of my thoughts, my unjust and uncharitable actions, and whatsoever I have transgressed against thee this day or at any time before. Behold, O God, my soul is troubled in the remembrance of my sins, in the frailty and sinfulness of my flesh exposed to every temptation, and of itself not able to resist any. Lord, God of mercy, I earnestly beg of thee to give me a great portion of thy grace, such as may be sufficient and effectual for the mortification of all my sins and vanities and disorders: that as I have formerly served my lust and unworthy desires, so now I may give myself wholly to thy service and the studies of a holy life.

✠ ✠

Blessed Lord, teach me frequently and sadly to remember my sins; and be thou pleased to remember them no more: let me never forget thy mercies, and do thou still remember to do me good. Teach me to walk always as in thy presence, ennoble my soul with great degrees of love to thee, and confine my spirit with great fear, religion, and veneration of thy holy name and laws; that it may become the great employment of my whole life to serve thee, to advance thy glory, to root out all the accurst habits of sin, that in holiness of life, in humility, in charity, in chastity, and in all the ornaments of grace, I may by patience wait for the coming of our Lord Jesus. AMEN.

✠ ✠

Teach me O Lord, to number my days that I may apply my heart unto wisdom, ever to remember my last end, that I may not dare to sin against thee. Let thy holy angels be ever present with me to keep me in all my ways from the malice and violence of the spirits of darkness, from evil company, and the occasions and opportunities of evil, from perishing in popular judgments, from all the ways of sinful shame, from the hands of all mine enemies, from a sinful life, and from despair in the day of my death. Then, O brightest Jesu, shine gloriously upon me, let thy mercies and the light of thy countenance sustain me in all my agonies, weaknesses and temptations. Give me opportunity of a prudent and spiritual guide, and of receiving the holy sacrament; and let thy loving Spirit so guide me in the ways of peace and safety, that with the testimony of a good conscience, and the sense of thy mercies and refreshment, I may depart this life in the unity of the church, in the love of God, and a certain hope of salvation through Jesus Christ our Lord and most blessed Savior. AMEN.

Our Father, etc.

✠ ✠

Another Form of Evening Prayer

Our Father, etc.

"I will lift up my eyes unto the hills from whence cometh my help," etc. (Ps. 121).

Glory be to the Father, etc.

Visit, I beseech thee, O Lord, this habitation with thy mercy, and me with thy grace and salvation. Let thy holy angels pitch their tents round about and dwell here, that no illusion of the night may abuse me, the spirits of darkness may not come near to hurt me, no evil or sad accident oppress me: and let the eternal Spirit of the Father dwell in my soul and body, filling every corner of my heart with light and grace. Let no deed of darkness overtake me; and let thy blessing, most blessed God, be upon me for ever, through Jesus Christ our Lord. AMEN.

✠ ✠

Into thy hands most blessed Jesu, I commend my soul and body, for thou hast redeemed both with thy most precious blood. So bless and sanctify my sleep unto me, that it may be temperate, holy and safe, a refreshment to my wearied body, to enable it so to serve my soul, that both may serve thee with a never failing duty. O let me never sleep in sin or death eternal, but give me a watchful and prudent spirit, that I may omit no opportunity of serving thee; that whether I sleep or wake, live or die, I may be thy servant and thy child; that when the work of my life is done, I may rest in the bosom of my Lord, till by the voice of the archangel, the trumpet of God, I shall be awakened and called to sit down and feast in the eternal supper of the Lamb. Grant this, O Lamb of God, for the honor of thy mercies, and the glory of thy name, O most merciful Savior and Redeemer Jesus. AMEN.

✠ ✠

Blessed be the God and Father of our Lord Jesus, who hath sent his angels, and kept me this day from the destruction that walketh at noon, and the arrow that flieth by day; and hath given me his Spirit to restrain me from those evils to which my own weaknesses, and my evil habits, and my unquiet enemies would easily betray me. Blessed and forever hallowed be thy name for that never ceasing shower of blessing by which I live, and am content and blest, and provided for in all necessities, and set forward in my duty and way to heaven. Blessing, honor, glory and power, be unto him that sitteth upon the throne, and to the Lamb, for ever and ever. AMEN.

Holy is our God. Holy is the Almighty. Holy is the Immortal. Holy, holy, holy, Lord God of Sabbaoth, have mercy upon me.

✠ ✠

Rules for the Practise of Prayer

1. We must be careful that we never ask anything of God that is sinful, or that directly ministers to sin: for that is to ask of God to dishonor himself, and to undo us. We had need consider what we pray; for before it returns in blessing, it must be joined with Christ's intercession, and presented to God. Let us principally ask of God power and assistance to do our duty, to glorify God, to do good works, to live a good life, to die in the fear and favor of God, and eternal life: these things God delights to give, and commands that we shall ask, and we may with confidence expect to be answered graciously: for these things are promised without any reservation of a secret condition; if we ask them and do our duty toward the obtaining them, we are sure never to miss them.

2. We may lawfully pray to God for the gifts of the Spirit that minister to holy ends, such as are the gift of preaching, the spirit of prayer, good expression, a ready and unloosed tongue, good understanding, learning, oppor-

tunities to publish them, etc., with these restraints. (1) That we can not be so confident of the event of these prayers as of the former. (2) That we must be curious to secure our intention in these desires, that we may not ask them to serve our own ends, but only for God's glory; and then we shall have them or a blessing for desiring them. In order to such purposes our intentions in the first desires can not be amiss, because they are able to sanctify other things, and therefore can not be unhallowed themselves. (3) We must submit to God's will, desiring him to choose our employment and to furnish our persons as he shall see expedient.

3. Whatsoever we may lawfully desire of temporal things, we may lawfully ask of God in prayer, and we may expect them as they are promised. (1) Whatsoever is necessary to our life and being is promised to us: and therefore we may with certainty expect food and raiment—food to keep us alive, clothing to keep us from nakedness and shame; so long as our life is permitted to us, so long all things necessary to our life shall be ministered. We may be secure of maintenance but not secure of our life, for that is promised, not this; only concerning food and raiment we are not to make accounts by the measure of our desires, but by the measure of

our needs. (2) Whatsoever is convenient for us, pleasant, and modestly delectable, we may pray for: so we do it (a) with submission to God's will; (b) without impatient desires; (c) that it be not a trifle and inconsiderable, but a matter so grave and concerning as to be a fit matter to be treated on between God and our souls; (d) that we ask it not to spend it upon our lusts, but for ends of justice, or charity, or religion, and that they be employed with sobriety.

4. He that would pray with effect, must live with care and piety (1 John 3:22; John 9:31; Isa. 1:15; 58:9; Mal. 2:10; 1 Tim. 2:8; Ps. 4:5; 66:8). For altho God gives to sinners and evil persons the common blessings of life and chance, yet either they want the comfort and blessing of those blessings, or they become occasions of sadder accidents to them, or serve to upbraid them in their ingratitude or irreligion: and in all cases they are not the effects of prayer, or the fruits of promise, or instances of a father's love; for they can not be expected with confidence, or received without danger, or used without a curse and mischief in their company. But as all sin is an impediment to prayer, so some have a special indisposition toward acceptation; such are uncharitableness and wrath; hypocrisy in the

present action, pride, and lust: because these, by defiling the body or the spirit, or by contradicting some necessary ingredients in prayer (such as are mercy, humility, purity, and sincerity), do defile the prayer and make it a direct sin in the circumstances or formality of the action.

5. All prayer must be made with faith and hope: that is, we must certainly believe we shall receive the grace which God hath commanded us to ask (Mark 11:24; James 1:6, 7); and we must hope for such things which he hath permitted us to ask; and our hope shall not be in vain, tho we miss what is not absolutely promised, because we shall at least have an equal blessing in the denial as in the grant. And therefore the former conditions must first be secured; that is, that we ask things necessary, or at least good and innocent and profitable, and that our persons be gracious in the eyes of God: or else what God hath promised to our natural needs he may in many degrees deny to our personal incapacity: but the thing being secured and the person disposed, there can be no fault at all; for whatsoever else remains is on God's part, and that can not possibly fail. But because the things which are not commanded can not possibly be secured (for we are not sure they are good in all circumstances), we can but hope for

such things even after we have secured our good intentions. We are sure of a blessing, but in what instance we are not yet assured.

6. Our prayers must be fervent, intense, earnest, and importunate, when we pray for things of high concernment and necessity. Continuing instant in prayer, striving in prayer, laboring fervently in prayer, night and day praying exceedingly, praying always with all prayer—so St. Paul calls it; watching unto prayer, so St. Peter; praying earnestly, so St. James (Rom. 12:12; 15:30; Col. 4:12; 1 Thess. 3:10; Eph. 6:8; 1 Pet. 4:7; James 5:16). And this is not to be abated in matters spiritual and of duty: for according as our desires are, so are our prayers; and as our prayers are, so shall be the grace; and as that is, so shall be the measure of glory. But this admits of degrees according to the perfection or imperfection of our state of life: but it hath no other measures, but ought to be as great as it can, the bigger the better; we must make no positive restraint upon ourselves. In other things we are to use a bridle; and as we must limit our desires with submission to God's will, so also we must limit the importunity of our prayers by the moderation and term of our desires. Pray for it as earnestly as you may desire it.

7. Our desires must be lasting, and our

prayers frequent, assiduous, and continual; not asking for a blessing once and then leaving it, but daily renewing our fruits, and exercising our hope, and faith, and patience, and long-suffering and religion, and resignation, and self-denial in all the degrees we shall be put to. This circumstance of duty our blessed Savior taught, saying that men "ought always to pray and not to faint" (Luke 18:1; 21:36). "Always to pray" signifies the frequent doing of the duty in general: but because we can not always ask several things, and we also have frequent need of the same thing, and those are such as concern our great interest, the precept comes home to this very circumstance, and St. Paul calls it "praying without ceasing" (1 Thess. 5:17), and himself in his own case gave a precedent, "For this case I besought the Lord thrice." And so did our blessed Lord; he went thrice to God on the same errand, with the same words, in a short space, about half a night; for his time to solicit his suit was but short. And the Philippians (Phil. 1:4) were remembered by the apostle, their spiritual father, always in every prayer of his. And thus we must always pray for the pardon of our sins, for the assistances of God's grace, for charity, for life eternal, never giving over till we die: and thus also we pray for supply of great temporal needs in their several proportions; in all cases, being curious, we do not give over out of weariness or impatience. For God oftentimes defers to grant our suit because he loves to hear us beg it, and hath a design to give us more than we ask, even a satisfaction of our desires and a blessing for the very importunity.

8. Let the words of our prayers be pertinent, grave, material, not studiously many, but according to our need, sufficient to express our wants and to signify our importunity. God hears us not the sooner for our many words, but much the sooner for an earnest desire; to which let apt and sufficient words minister, be they few or many according as it happens. A long prayer and a short differ not in their capacities of being accepted; for both of them take their value according to the fervency of spirit and the charity of the prayer. That prayer which is short, by reason of an impatient spirit, or dulness, or despite of holy things, or indifferency of desires, is very often criminal, always imperfect; and that prayer which is long out of ostentation, or superstition, or a trifling spirit, is as criminal and imperfect as the other in their several instances. This rule relates to private prayer. In public our devotion is to be measured by the appointed office, and we are to support

our spirit with spiritual arts, that our private
spirit may be a part of the public spirit, and
be adopted into the society and blessings of
the communion of saints.

9. In all forms of prayer mingle petition
with thanksgiving, that you may endear the
present prayer and the future blessing by returning praise and thanks for what we have already received. This is St. Paul's advice: "Be
careful for nothing, but in every thing by
prayer and supplication with thanksgiving let
your requests be made known unto God"
(Phil. 4: 6).

10. Whatever we beg of God, let us also
work for it, if the thing be matter of duty or
a consequent to industry. For God loves to
bless labor and to reward it, but not to support idleness.   And therefore our blessed
Savior in his sermons joins watchfulness with
prayer: for God's graces are but assistances,
not new creations of the whole habit in every
instant or period of our life.   Read scriptures
and then pray to God for understanding.
Pray against temptation; but you must also
resist the devil, and then he will flee from you.
Ask of God competency of living; but you
must also work with your hands the things that
are honest, that ye may have to supply in time
of need.   We can but do our endeavor and
pray for a blessing, and then leave the success

with God: and beyond this we can not deliberate, we can not take care: but so far we must.

11. To this purpose let every man study his prayers, and read his duty in his petitions. For the body of our prayer is the sum of our duty: and as we must ask of God whatsoever we need, so we must labor for all that we ask. Because it is our duty, therefore we must pray for God's grace: because God's grace is necessary, and without it we can do nothing, we are sufficiently taught that in the proper matter of our religious prayers is the just matter of our duty: and if we shall turn our prayers into precepts, we shall the easier turn our hearty desires into effective practises.

12. In all our prayers we must be careful to attend our present work, having a present mind, not wandering upon impertinent things, not distant from our words, much less contrary to them: and if our thoughts do at any time wander and divert upon other objects, bring them back again with prudent and severe arts; by all means striving to obtain a diligent, a sober, an untroubled and a composed spirit.

13. Let your posture and gesture of body in prayers be reverent, grave and humble, according to public order or the best examples; if it be in public, if it be in private, either

stand or kneel, or lie flat upon the ground on your face, in your ordinary and more solemn prayers, but in extraordinary, casual, and ejaculatory prayers, the reverence and devotion of the soul and the lifting up the eyes and hands to God with any other posture, not indecent, is usual and commendable; for we may pray in bed, on horseback, everywhere and at all times (1 Tim. 2:8), and in all circumstances, and it is well if we do so; and some servants have not an opportunity to pray so often as they would, unless they supply the appetites of religion by such accidental devotions.

14. "Let prayers and supplications, and giving of thanks, be made for all men: for kings and all that are in authority. For this is good and acceptable in the sight of God our Savior" (1 Tim. 2:2). We who must love our neighbors as ourselves, must also pray for them as for ourselves, with this only difference —that we may enlarge in our temporal desires for kings, and pray for secular prosperity to them with more importunity than for ourselves, because they need more to enable their duty and government, and for the interests of religion and justice. This part of prayer is by the apostle called "intercession," in which with special care we are to remember our relatives, our family, our charge, our

benefactors, our creditors; not forgetting to beg pardon and charity for our enemies, and protection against them.

15. Rely not on a single prayer in matters of great concernment, but make it as public as you can by obtaining of others to pray for you; this being the great blessing of the communion of saints, that a prayer united is strong, like a well-ordered army, and God loves to be tied fast with such cords of love and constrained by a holy violence.

16. Every time that is not seized upon by some other duty is seasonable enough for prayer; but let it be performed as a solemn duty morning and evening, that God may begin and end all our business, and the outgoings of the morning and the evening may praise him; for so we bless God, and God blesses us. And yet fail not to find or make opportunities to worship God at some other times of the day—at least by ejaculations and short addresses, more or less, longer or shorter, solemnly or without solemnity, privately or publicly, as you can·or are permitted: always remembering that as every sin is a degree of danger and unsafety, so every pious prayer and well-employed opportunity is a degree of return to hope and pardon.

A Prayer of John Austin

O God, our heavenly Father, who hast commanded us to love one another as thy children, and hast ordained the highest friendship in the bond of thy Spirit, we beseech thee to maintain and preserve us always in the same bond, to thy glory and our mutual comfort, with all those to whom we are bound by any special tie, either of nature or of choice; that we may be perfected together in that love which is from above, and which never faileth when all other things shall fail. Send down the dew of thy heavenly grace upon us, that we may have joy in each other that passeth not away; and, having lived together in love here, according to thy commandment, may live forever together with them, being made one in thee, in thy glorious kingdom hereafter, through Jesus Christ our Lord. AMEN.

SELECTIONS FROM

The Saints' Everlasting Rest

BY

RICHARD BAXTER

RICHARD BAXTER

Author of "The Saints' Everlasting Rest" (1650), "Call to the Unconverted" (1657), and "The Reformed Pastor" (1656), and one of the most eminent of English Non-conformist divines, was born at Rowton, Shropshire, November 12, 1615, and died in London December 8, 1691. From his earliest days his disposition was religious. Tho without a university education, his health never being robust, by application he acquired great learning. He was ordained into the ministry of the Church of England, altho some Non-conformist views received his sanction. For two years, 1640-42, he officiated for the vicar of Kidderminster. At the outbreak of the Civil War in 1642, being at variance with public feeling in Worcestershire, he ministered for two years to the garrison and inhabitants of Coventry. His sympathies were almost wholly Puritan, and after Naseby he was chaplain to a regiment, and was present at several sieges. During this period he sought, with considerable success, to moderate the extreme views, political and religious, of the soldiers. At the Restoration he became a chaplain of the king, took a leading part in the Savoy Conference, and declined the bishopric of Hereford. He left the Church of England just before the passage of the Act of Uniformity, and retired to Acton, Middlesex. He continued to preach, often to great multitudes, in the face of persecution, being twice imprisoned, once for eighteen months under the notorious Jeffreys. In this period his distinctively theological works were composed. His fame rests, however, upon the practical works named above.

Introduction, With Some Account of the Nature of the Saints' Rest

[There remaineth therefore a rest unto the people of God.—Heb. 4 : 9.]

It was not only our interest in God, and actual enjoyment of him, which was lost in Adam's fall, but all spiritual knowledge of him, and true disposition toward such a felicity. When the Son of God comes with recovering grace and discoveries of a spiritual and eternal happiness and glory, he finds not faith in man to believe it. As the poor man, that would not believe any one had such a sum as a hundred pounds, it was so far above what himself possest, so men will hardly now believe there is such a happiness as once they had, much less as Christ hath now procured, when God would give the Israelites his Sabbaths of rest in a land of rest, it was harder to make them believe it than to overcome their enemies and procure it for them. And when they had it, only as a small intimation and earnest of an incomparably more glorious rest through Christ, they yet believe no more than they possess, but say, with the epicure at the feast, Sure there is no other heaven but this! or, if they expect more by

71

the Messiah, it is only the increase of their earthly felicity. The apostle aims most of this epistle against this obduracy, and clearly and largely proves that the end of all ceremonies and shadows is to direct them to Jesus Christ, the substance; and that the rest of Sabbaths and Canaan should teach them to look for a further rest, which indeed is their happiness. My text is his conclusion after divers arguments; a conclusion which contains the ground of all the believers' comfort, the end of all his duty and sufferings, the life and sum of all gospel promises and Christian privileges.

What more welcome to men under personal afflictions, tiring duties, disappointments, or sufferings, than rest? It is not our comfort only, but our stability. Our liveliness in all duties, our enduring of tribulation, our honoring of God, the vigor of our love, thankfulness and all our graces; yea, the very being of our religion and Christianity depend on the believing, serious thoughts of our rest. And now, reader, whoever thou art, young or old, rich or poor, I entreat thee and charge thee, in the name of thy Lord, who will shortly call thee to a reckoning and judge thee to thy everlasting, unchangeable state, that thou give not these things the reading only, and so dismiss them with a bare approbation;

but that thou set upon this work, and take
God in Christ for thy only rest, and fix thy
heart upon him above all. May the living
God, who is the portion and rest of his saints,
make these our carnal minds so spiritual, and
our earthly hearts so heavenly, that loving
him and delighting in him may be the work
of our lives; and that neither I that write nor
you that read this book may ever be turned
from this path of life; "lest, a promise being
left us of entering into his rest," we should
"come short of it," through our own unbelief
or negligence.

The saints' rest is the most happy state of a
Christian; or, it is the perfect endless enjoyment of God by the perfected saints, according
to the measure of their capacity, to which
their souls arrive at death, and both soul and
body most fully after the resurrection and
final judgment.

There are some things necessarily presup-
posed in the nature of this rest: as,

That mortal men are the persons seeking it.
For angels and glorified spirits have it already, and the devils and damned are past
hope:

That they choose God only for their end
and happiness. He that takes any thing else
for his happiness is out of the way the first
step:

That they are distant from this end. This is the woful case of all mankind since the fall. When Christ comes with regenerating grace, he finds no man sitting still, but all posting to eternal ruin and making haste toward hell; till by conviction he first brings them to a stand, and then by conversion turns their hearts and lives sincerely to himself. This end, and its excellency, is supposed to be known and seriously intended. An unknown good moves not to desire or endeavor. And not only a distance from this rest, but the true knowledge of this distance, is also supposed. They that never yet knew they were without God, and in the way to hell, never yet knew the way to heaven. Can a man find he hath lost his God and his soul, and not cry, I am undone? The reason why so few obtain this rest is they will not be convinced that they are, in point of title, distant from it, and, in point of practise, contrary to it. Who ever sought for that which he knew not he had lost? "They that be whole need not a physician, but they that are sick":

The influence of a superior moving Cause is also supposed; else we shall all stand still, and not move toward our rest. If God move us not, we can not move. It is a most necessary part of our Christian wisdom to keep our subordination to God and dependence on him. "We are not sufficient of ourselves to think any thing as of ourselves, but our sufficiency is of God." "Without me," says Christ, "ye can do nothing."

It is next supposed, that they who seek this rest have an inward principle of spiritual life. God does not move men like stones, but he endows them with life, not to enable them to move without him, but in subordination to himself, the first Mover.

And further, this rest supposes such an actual tendency of soul toward it as is regular and constant, earnest and laborious. He that hides his talent shall receive the wages of a slothful servant. Christ is the door, the only way to this rest. "But strait is the gate and narrow is the way"; and we must strive, if we will enter; for "many will seek to enter in, and shall not be able"; which implies, "that the kingdom of heaven suffereth violence." Nor will it bring us to the end of the saints, if we begin in the spirit and end in the flesh. He only "that endureth to the end shall be saved." And never did a soul obtain rest with God whose desire was not set upon him above all things else in the world. "Where your treasure is, there will your heart be also." The remainder of our old nature will much weaken and interrupt these desires, but never overcome them. And, considering the opposition to our desires, from the contrary principles in our nature, and from the weakness of our graces, together with our continued distance from the end, our tendency to that end must be laborious, and with all our might. All these things are pre-supposed, in order to a Christian's obtaining an interest in heavenly rest.

Now we have ascended these steps into the outward court, may we look within the veil? May we show what this rest contains, as well as what it presupposes? Alas! how little know I of that glory! The glimpse which Paul had, contained what could not, or must not, be uttered. Had he spoken the things of heaven in the language of heaven, and none understood that language, what the better? The Lord reveal to me what I may reveal to you! The Lord open some light, and show both you and me our inheritance! Not as to Balaam only, whose eyes were opened to see the goodliness of Jacob's tent and Israel's tabernacles, where he had no portion, and from whence must come his own destruction; not as to Moses, who had only a discovery instead of possession, and saw the land which he never entered; but as the pearl was revealed to the merchant in the gospel, who rested not till he had sold all he had and bought it; and as heaven was opened to blessed

Stephen, which he was shortly to enter, and the glory showed him which should be his own possession!

The things contained in heavenly rest are such as these: a ceasing from means of grace; a perfect freedom from all evils; the highest degree of the saints' personal perfection, both of body and soul; the nearest enjoyment of God, the chief good; and a sweet and constant action of all the powers of body and soul in this enjoyment of God.

1. One thing contained in heavenly rest is the ceasing from means of grace. When we have obtained the haven, we have done sailing. When the workman receives his wages, it is implied he has done his work. When we are at our journey's end, we have done with the way. Whether prophecies, they shall fail; whether tongues, they shall cease; whether knowledge, it also, so far as it had the nature of means, shall vanish away. There shall be no more prayer, because no more necessity, but the full enjoyment of what we prayed for: neither shall we need to fast, and weep, and watch any more, being out of the reach of sin and temptations. Preaching is done; the ministry of man ceases; ordinances become useless; the laborers are called in, because the harvest is gathered, the tares burned, and the work finished; the un-

regenerate past hope, and the saints past fear, for ever.

2. There is in heavenly rest a perfect freedom from all evils: from all the evils that accompanied us through our course, and which necessarily follow our absence from the chief good, besides our freedom from those eternal flames and restless miseries which the neglectors of Christ and grace must for ever endure; a woful inheritance, which, both by birth and actual merit, was due to us as well as to them! In heaven there is nothing that defileth or is unclean. All that remains without. And doubtless there is not such a thing as grief and sorrow known there; nor is there such a thing as a pale face, a languid body, feeble joints, helpless infancy, decrepit age, peccant humors, painful or pining sickness, griping fears, consuming cares, not whatsoever deserves the name of evil. We wept and lamented when the world rejoiced; but our sorrow is turned to joy, and our joy shall no man take from us.

3. Another ingredient of this rest is, the highest degree of the saints' personal perfection, both of body and soul. Were the glory ever so great, and themselves not made capable of it by a personal perfection suitable thereto, it would be little to them. "Eye hath not seen, nor ear heard, neither

have entered into the heart of man, the things which God hath prepared for them that love him.'' For the eye of flesh is not capable of seeing them, nor this ear of hearing them, nor this heart of understanding them: but there, the eye, and ear, and heart are made capable; else, how do they enjoy them? The more perfect the sight is, the more delightful the beautiful object. The more perfect the appetite, the sweeter the food. The more musical the ear, the more pleasant the melody. The more perfect the soul, the more joyous those joys, and the more glorious to us is that glory.

4. The principal part of this rest is our nearest enjoyment of God, the chief good. And here, reader, wonder not if I be at a loss, and if my apprehensions receive but little of that which is in my expressions. If it did not appear to the beloved disciple what we shall be, but only, in general, "that when Christ shall appear we shall be like him," no wonder if I know little. When I know so little of God, I can not much know what it is to enjoy him. If I know so little of spirits, how little of the Father of pirits, or the state of my own soul, when advanced to the enjoyment of him! I stand and look upon a heap of ants, and see them all at one view: they know not me, my being, nature, or thoughts,

tho I am their fellow-creature: how little, then, must we know of the great Creator, tho he, with one view, clearly beholds us all! A glimpse, the saints behold as in a glass, which makes us capable of some poor, dark apprehensions of what we shall behold in glory. If I should tell a worldling what the holiness and spiritual joys of the saints on earth are, he can not know; for grace can not be clearly known without grace; how much less could he conceive it, should I tell him of this glory! But to the saints I may be somewhat more encouraged to speak, for grace gives them a dark knowledge and slight taste of glory.

If men and angels should study to speak the blessedness of that state in one word, what could they say beyond this, that it is the nearest enjoyment of God? O the full joys offered to a believer in that one sentence of Christ, "Father, I will that they whom thou hast given me be with me where I am, that they may behold my glory which thou hast given me!" Every word is full of life and joy. If the Queen of Sheba had cause to say of Solomon's glory, "Happy are thy men, happy are these thy servants, who stand continually before thee, and hear thy wisdom"; then, surely, they that stand continually before God, and see his glory, and the glory of

Richard Baxter

the Lamb, are more than happy. To them will Christ give to eat of the tree of life, and to eat of the hidden manna; yea, he will make them pillars in the temple of God, and they shall go no more out; and he will write upon them the name of his God, and the name of the city of his God, which is New Jerusalem, which cometh down out of heaven from his God, and he will write upon them his new name; yea, more, if more may be, he will grant them to sit with him in his throne. "These are they who came out of great tribulation, and have washed their robes, and made them white in the blood of the Lamb; therefore are they before the throne of God, and serve him day and night in his temple, and he that sitteth on the throne shall dwell among them. The Lamb, which is in the midst of the throne, shall feed them, and shall lead them unto living fountains of water; and God shall wipe away all tears from their eyes." O blind, deceived world! can you show us such a glory? This is the city of our God, where the tabernacle of God is with men, and he will dwell with them, and they shall be his people, and God himself shall be with them, and be their God. The glory of God shall lighten it, and the Lamb is the light thereof. And there shall be no more curse; but the throne of God and of the

Lamb shall be in it; and his servants shall serve him, and they shall see his face, and his name shall be in their foreheads. These sayings are faithful and true, and the things which must shortly be done.

And now we say, as Mephibosheth, let the world take all, forasmuch as our Lord will come in peace. Rejoice, therefore, in the Lord, O ye righteous! and say, with his servant David, "The Lord is the portion of mine inheritance: the lines are fallen unto me in pleasant places; yea, I have a goodly heritage. I have set the Lord always before me; because he is at my right hand, I shall not be moved. Therefore my heart is glad, and my glory rejoiceth; my flesh also shall rest in hope. For thou wilt not leave my soul in hell, neither wilt thou suffer thine Holy One to see corruption. Thou wilt show me the path of life; in thy presence is fulness of joy; at thy right hand there are pleasures for evermore." What presumption would it have been, once, to have thought or spoken of such a thing, if God had not spoken it before us! I durst not have thought of the saints' preferment in this life, as Scripture sets it forth, had it not been the express truth of God. How unbecoming to talk of being sons of God—speaking to him, having fellowship with him, dwelling in him and he in us—if this had not been God's own language! How much less durst we have once thought of shining forth as the sun, of being joint heirs with Christ, of judging the world, of sitting on Christ's throne, of being one in him and the Father, if we had not all this from the mouth, and under the hand of God! But hath he said, and shall he not do it? Hath he spoken, and shall he not make it good?—Yes, as the Lord God is true, thus shall it be done to the man whom Christ delighteth to honor.

Be of good cheer, Christian; the time is at hand when God and thou shalt be near, and as near as thou canst well desire. Thou shalt dwell in his family. Is that enough? It is better to be "a door-keeper in the house of God, than to dwell in the tents of wickedness." Thou shalt ever stand before him, about his throne, in the room with him, in his presence-chamber. Wouldst thou yet be nearer? Thou shalt be his child, and he thy Father; thou shalt be an heir to his kingdom; yea, more, the spouse of his Son. And what more canst thou desire? Thou shalt be a member of the body of his Son; he shall be thy Head; thou shalt be one with him, who is one with the Father, as he himself hath desired for thee of his Father: "That they all may be one, as thou, Father, art in me, and I in thee, that they also may be one

in us; and the glory which thou gavest me, I
have given them, that they may be one, even
as we are one; I in them, and thou in me,
that they may be made perfect in one, and
that the world may know that thou hast sent
me, and hast loved them as thou hast loved
me.''

5. We must add, that this rest contains a
sweet and constant action of all the powers of
the soul and body in this enjoyment of God.
It is not the rest of a stone, which ceaseth
from all motion when it attains the center.
This body shall be so changed that it shall no
more be flesh and blood, which can not inherit
the kingdom of God; but a spiritual body.
We sow not that body which shall be, but
God giveth it a body as it hath pleased him,
and to every seed his own body. If grace
makes a Christian differ so much from what
he was as to say, I am not the man I was;
how much more will glory make us differ! As
much as a body spiritual, above the sun in
glory, exceeds these frail, noisome, diseased
bodies of flesh, so far shall our senses exceed
those we now possess. Doubtless, as God
advances our senses and enlarges our capacity, so will he advance the happiness of those
senses, and fill up, with himself, all that capacity. Certainly the body would not be raised
up and continued, if it were not to share

in the glory. As it hath shared in the obedience and sufferings, so shall it also in the blessedness. As Christ bought the whole man, so shall the whole partake of the everlasting benefits of the purchase. O blessed employment of a glorified body! to stand before the throne of God and the Lamb, and to sound forth for ever, "Thou art worthy, O Lord, to receive glory, and honor, and power. Worthy is the Lamb that was slain, to receive power, and riches, and wisdom, and strength, and honor, and glory, and blessing; for thou hast redeemed us to God, by thy blood, out of every kindred, and tongue, and people, and nation; and hast made us unto our God kings and priests. Alleluia: salvation, and glory, and honor, and power, unto the Lord our God. Alleluia, for the Lord God omnipotent reigneth." O Christians! this is the blessed rest; a rest, as it were, without rest; for "they rest not day and night, saying, Holy, holy, holy Lord God Almighty, who was, and is, and is to come." And if the body shall be thus employed, O how shall the soul be taken up! As its powers and capacities are greatest, so its actions are strongest, and its enjoyments sweetest. As the bodily senses have their proper actions, whereby they receive and enjoy their objects, so does the soul in its own actions enjoy its own objects by knowing, remembering, loving, and delightful joying. This is the soul's enjoyment. By these eyes it sees, and by these arms it embraces.

Knowledge, of itself, is very desirable. As far as the rational soul exceeds the sensitive, so far the delights of a philosopher, in discovering the secrets of nature and knowing the mystery of sciences, exceed the delights of the drunkard, the voluptuary, or the sensualist. So excellent is all truth. What, then, is their delight who know the God of truth! How noble a faculty of the soul is the understanding! It can compass the earth; it can measure the sun, moon, stars, and heaven; it can foreknow each eclipse to a minute, many years before. But this is the top of all its excellency, that it can know God, who is infinite, who made all these—a little here, and more, much more, hereafter. O the wisdom and goodness of our blessed Lord! He hath created the understanding with a natural bias and inclination to truth, as its object; and to the prime truth, as its prime object. Christian, when, after long gazing heavenward, thou hast got a glimpse of Christ, dost thou not sometimes seem to have been with Paul in the third heaven, whether in the body or out, and to have seen what is unutterable? Art thou not, with Peter, ready to say, "Master, it is good to be here"? "O that I might dwell in this mount! O that I might ever see what I now see!" Didst thou never look so long upon the Sun of Righteousness till thine eyes were dazzled with his astonishing glory? And did not the splendor of it make all things below seem dark and drear to thee? Especially in the day of suffering for Christ, when he usually appears most manifestly to his people, didst thou never see one walking in the midst of the fiery furnace with thee, like the Son of God? Believe me, Christians, yea, believe God; you that have known most of God in Christ here, it is as nothing to what you shall know: in comparison of that it scarce deserves to be called knowledge. For as these bodies, so that knowledge must cease, that a more perfect may succeed. "Knowledge shall vanish away. For we know in part. But when that which is perfect is come, then that which is in part shall be done away. When I was a child, I spake as a child, I understood as a child, I thought as a child; but, when I became a man, I put away childish things. For now we see through a glass darkly, but then face to face; now I know in part, but then shall I know even as also I am known." Marvel not, therefore, Christian, how it can be life eternal to know God and

Jesus Christ. To enjoy God and Christ is eternal life; and the soul's enjoying is in knowing. They that savor only of earth and consult with flesh think it a poor happiness to know God. "But we know that we are of God, and the whole world lieth in wickedness; and we know that the Son of God is come, and hath given us an understanding, that we may know him that is true; and we are in him that is true, even in his Son Jesus Christ. This is the true God and eternal life."

The memory will not be idle, or useless, in this blessed work. From that height the saint can look behind him and before him. And to compare past with present things must raise in the blessed soul an inconceivable esteem and sense of its condition. To stand on that mount, whence we can see the wilderness and Canaan both at once; to stand in heaven and look back on earth, and weigh them together in the balance of a comparing sense and judgment, how must it needs transport the soul, and make it cry out.

"Is this the purchase that cost so dear as the blood of Christ? No wonder. O blessed price! and thrice blessed love, that invented and condescended! Is this the end of believing? Is this the end of the Spirit's workings? Have the gales of grace blown me into such a harbor? Is it hither that Christ hath allured

my soul? O blessed way, and thrice blessed
end! Is this the glory which the Scriptures
spoke of, and ministers preached of so much?
I see the gospel is indeed good tidings, even
tidings of peace and good things, tidings of
great joy to all nations! Is my mourning, my
fasting, my sad humblings, my heavy walking, come to this? Is my praying, watching,
fearing to offend, come to this? Are all my
afflictions, Satan's temptations, the world's
scorns and jeers, come to this? O vile nature,
that resisted so much and so long such a
blessing! Unworthy soul! is this the place
thou camest to so unwillingly? Was duty
wearisome? Was the world too good to lose?
Couldst thou not leave all, deny all, and suffer any thing for this? Was thou loath to die,
to come to this? O false heart, thou hadst
almost betrayed me to eternal flames, and
lost me this glory? Art thou not now ashamed, my soul, that ever thou didst question
that love which brought thee hither? that
thou wast jealous of the faithfulness of thy
Lord? that thou suspectedst his love, when
thou shouldst only have suspected thyself?
that ever thou didst quench a motion of his
Spirit? and that thou shouldst misinterpret
those providences, and repine at those ways
which have such an end? Now thou art sufficiently convinced that thy blessed Redeemer

was saving thee, as well when he crossed thy
desires, as when he granted them; when he
broke thy heart, as when he bound it up. No
thanks to thee, unworthy self, for this received crown; but to Jehovah and the Lamb
be glory for ever.''

But, O! the full, the near, the sweet enjoyment, is that of love. ''God is love, and he
that dwelleth in love dwelleth in God, and
God in him.'' Now the poor soul complains
''O that I could love Christ more!'' Then
thou canst not but love him. Now, thou
knowest little of his amiableness and therefore lovest little: then, thine eyes will affect
thy heart, and the continual viewing of that
perfect beauty will keep thee in continual
transports of love. Christians, doth it not
now stir up your love to remember all the
experiences of his love? Doth not kindness
melt you, and the sunshine of divine goodness
warm your frozen hearts? What will it do
then, when you shall live in love, and have
all in him, who is all? Surely love is both
work and wages. What a high favor, that
God will give us leave to love him! that he
will be embraced by those who have embraced
lust and sin before him! But more than
this, he returneth love for love; nay, a thousand times more. Christian, thou wilt be
then brimful of love; yet, love as much as

thou canst, thou shalt be ten thousand times more beloved. Were the arms of the Son of God open upon the cross, and an open passage made to his heart by the spear; and will not his arms and heart be open to thee in glory? Did not he begin to love before thou lovedst, and will not he continue now? Did he love thee, an enemy? thee, a sinner? thee, who even loathedst thyself? and own thee, when thou didst disclaim thyself? And will he not now immeasurably love thee, a son? thee, a perfect saint? thee, who returnest some love for love? He that in love wept over the old Jerusalem when near its ruin, with what love will he rejoice over the new Jerusalem in her glory!

Christian, believe this, and think on it: thou shalt be eternally embraced in the arms of that love which was from everlasting, and will extend to everlasting; of that love which brought the Son of God's love from heaven to earth, from earth to the cross, from the cross to the grave, from the grave to glory; that love which was weary, hungry, tempted, scorned, scourged, buffeted, spit upon, crucified, pierced; which did fast, pray, teach, heal, weep, sweat, bleed, die; that love will eternally embrace thee. When perfect created love and most perfect uncreated love meet together, it will not be like Joseph and his brethren, who lay upon one another's necks weeping; it will be loving and rejoicing, not loving and sorrowing. Yes, it will make Satan's court ring with the news that Joseph's brethren are come, that the saints are arrived safe at the bosom of Christ, out of the reach of hell for ever. Nor is there any such love as David's and Jonathan's, breathing out its last into sad lamentations for a forced separation. Know this, believer, to thy everlasting comfort, if those arms have once embraced thee, neither sin nor hell can get thee thence for ever. Thou hast not to deal with an inconstant creature, but with him with whom is no variableness nor shadow of turning. His love to thee will not be as thine was on earth to him, seldom, and cold, up, and down. He that would not cease nor abate his love for all thine enmity, unkind neglects, and churlish resistances, can he cease to love thee when he hath made thee truly lovely? He that keepeth thee so constant in thy love to him that thou canst challenge tribulation, distress, persecution, famine, nakedness, peril, or sword to separate thy love from Christ, how much more will he himself be constant! Indeed thou mayest be "persuaded that neither death nor life, nor angels, nor principalities, nor powers, nor things present, nor things to come, nor height, nor depth, nor any other creature, shall be able to separate us from the love of God which is in Christ Jesus our Lord." And now, are we not left in the apostle's admiration: "What shall we say to these things?" Infinite love must needs be mystery to a finite capacity. No wonder angels desire to look into this mystery. And if it be the study of saints here "to know the breadth, and length, and depth, and height of the love of Christ, which passeth knowledge"; the saints' everlasting rest must consist in the enjoyment of God by love.

Nor does joy share least in this fruition. It is this which all we have mentioned lead to, and conclude in; even the inconceivable complacency which the blessed feel in seeing, knowing, loving, and being beloved of God. This is "the white stone which no man knoweth, saving he that receiveth it." Surely this is the joy with which a stranger doth not intermeddle. All Christ's ways of mercy tend to and end in the saints' joys. He wept, sorrowed, suffered, that they might rejoice; he sends the Spirit to be their comforter; he multiplies promises; he discovers their future happiness, that their joy may be full. He opens to them the fountain of living waters, that they may thirst no more, and that it may spring up in them to everlasting life. He chastens them that he may give them rest. He makes it their duty to rejoice in him always, and again commands them to rejoice. He never brings them into so low a condition that he does not leave them more cause of joy than sorrow. And hath the Lord such a care of our comfort here? O what will that joy be where, the soul being perfectly prepared for joy and joy prepared by Christ for the soul, it shall be our work, our business, eternally to rejoice! It seems the saints' joy shall be greater than the damned's torment; for their torment is the torment of creatures, prepared for the devil and his angels; but our joy is the joy of our Lord. The same glory which the Father gave the Son, the Son hath given them, to sit with him in his throne, even as he is set down with his Father in his throne. Thou, poor soul, who prayest for joy, waitest for joy, complainest for want of joy, longest for joy; thou then shalt have full joy, as much as thou canst hold, and more than ever thou thoughtest on, or thy heart desired. In the meantime walk carefully, watch constantly, and then let God measure out to thee thy times and degrees of joy. It may be he keeps them until thou hast more need. Thou hadst better lose thy comfort than thy safety. If thou shouldst die full of fears and sorrows, it will be but a moment, and they are all gone and concluded in joy inconceivable. As the joy of the hypocrite, so the fears of the upright are but for a moment. God's "anger endureth but a moment; in his favor is life; weeping may endure for a night, but joy cometh in the morning." O blessed morning! Poor, humble, drooping soul, how would it fill thee with joy now, if a voice from heaven should tell thee of the love of God, the pardon of thy sins, and assure thee of thy part in these joys! What then will thy joy be, when thy actual possession shall convince thee of thy title, and thou shalt be in heaven before thou art well aware!

And it is not thy joy only; it is a mutual joy as well as a mutual love. Is there joy in heaven at thy conversion, and will there be none at thy glorification? Will not the angels welcome thee thither, and congratulate thy safe arrival? Yes, it is the joy of Jesus Christ; for now he hath the end of his undertaking, labor, suffering, dying, when we have our joys; when he is "glorified in his Saints, and admired in all them that believe"; when he "sees of the travail of his soul, and is satisfied." This is Christ's harvest, when he shall reap the fruit of his labors; and it will not repent him concerning his sufferings, but he will rejoice over his purchased inheritance, and his people will rejoice in him. Yea, the Father himself puts on joy, too, in our joy. As we grieve his Spirit and weary him with our iniquities, so he is rejoiced in our good. O how quickly does he now spy a returning prodigal, even afar off! How does he run and meet him! And with what compassion does he fall on his neck and kiss him, and put on him the best robe, and a ring on his hand, and shoes on his feet, and kills the fatted calf, to eat and be merry! This is indeed a happy meeting; but nothing to the embracing and joy of that last and great meeting. Yea, more; as God doth mutually love and joy, so he makes this his rest, as it is our rest. What an eternal Sabbatism, when the work of redemption, sanctification, preservation, glorification, is all finished and perfected for ever! "The Lord thy God in the midst of thee is mighty; he will save, he will rejoice over thee with joy, he will rest in his love, he will joy over thee with singing." Well may we then rejoice in our God with joy, and rest in our love, and joy in him with singing.

Alas! my fearful heart scarce dares proceed. Methinks I hear the Almighty's voice saying to me, "Who is this that darkeneth counsel by words without knowledge?" But pardon thy servant, O Lord. I have not pried into unrevealed things. I bewail that my apprehensions are so dull, my thoughts so mean, my affections so stupid, and my expressions so low and unbecoming such a glory. I have only heard by the hearing of the ear: O let thy servant see thee, and possess these joys; then shall I have more suitable conceptions, and shall give thee fuller glory; I shall abhor my present self, and disclaim and renounce all these imperfections. "I have uttered that I understood not, things too wonderful for me, which I knew not." Yet "I believed, and therefore have I spoken." What, Lord, canst thou expect from dust, but levity? or from corruption, but defilement? Tho the weakness and irreverence be the fruit of my own corruption, yet the fire is from thine altar, and the work of thy commanding. I looked not into thy ark, nor put forth my hand unto it without thee. Wash away these stains also in the blood of the Lamb. Imperfect or none must be thy service here. O take thy Son's excuse, "the spirit is willing, but the flesh is weak."

[Following chapters deal with the great preparatives to the saints' rest, its excellencies, character of those for whom it is designed, the misery of those who lose it, the necessity of diligently seeking it, how to discern our title to it, duty of seeking it, and that it is not to be expected on earth.]

The Importance of Leading a Heavenly Life Upon Earth

Is there such a rest remaining for us? Why, then, are not our thoughts more upon it? Why are not our hearts continually there? Why dwell we not there in constant contemplation? What is the cause of this neglect? Are we reasonable in this, or are we not? Hath the eternal God provided us such a glory, and promised to take us up to dwell with himself? and is not this worth thinking on? Should not the strongest desires of our hearts be after it? Do we believe this, and yet forget and neglect it? If God will not give us leave to approach this light, what mean all his earnest invitations? Why doth he so condemn our earthly-mindedness, and command us to set our affections on things above? Ah, vile hearts! Were God against it, we were likelier to be for it; but when he commands our hearts to heaven, then they will not stir one inch: like our predecessors, the sinful Israelites, when God would have them march for Canaan, then they mutiny and will not stir; but when God bids them not go, then will they be presently marching. If God say, "Love not the world, nor the things of the world," we dote upon it. How freely, how frequently can we think of our pleasures, our friends, our labors, our flesh and its lusts! yea, our wrongs and miseries, our fears and sufferings! But where is the Christian whose heart is on his rest? What is the matter? Are we so full of joy that we need no more? Or is there nothing in heaven for our joyous thoughts? Or rather, are not our hearts carnal and stupid? Let us humble these sensual hearts, that have in them no more of Christ and glory. If this world was the only subject of our discourse, all would call us ungodly; why, then, may we not call our hearts ungodly, that have so little delight in Christ and heaven?

But I am speaking only to those whose portion is in heaven, whose hopes are there, and who have forsaken all to enjoy this glory; and shall I be discouraged from persuading such to be heavenly-minded? Fellow Christians, if you will not hear and obey, who will? Well may we be discouraged to exhort the blind, ungodly world, and may say, as Moses did, "Behold, the children of Israel have not hearkened unto me; how then shall Pharaoh hear me?" I require thee, reader, as ever thou hopest for a part in this glory, that thou presently take thy heart to task, chide it for its wilful strangeness to God, turn thy thoughts from the pursuit of vanity, bend thy soul to study eternity, busy it about the life to come, habituate thyself to such contemplations, and let not those thoughts be seldom and cursory, but bathe thy soul in heaven's delights; and if thy backward soul begin to flag and thy thoughts to scatter, call them back, hold them to their work, bear not with their laziness, nor connive at one neglect. And when thou hast, in obedience to God, tried this work, got acquainted with it, and kept a guard on thy thoughts till they are accustomed to obey, thou wilt then find thyself in the suburbs of heaven, and that there is indeed a sweetness in the work and way of God, and that the life of Christianity is a life of joy. Thou wilt meet with those abundant consolations which thou hast prayed, panted, and groaned after, and which so few Christians do ever here obtain, because they know not this way to them, or else make not conscience of walking in it.

Say not, "We are unable to set our own hearts on heaven; this must be the work of God only." Tho God be the chief disposer of your hearts, yet, next under him, you have the greatest command of them yourself. Tho without Christ you can do nothing, yet under him you may do much, and must, or else it will be undone and yourselves undone through your neglect. Christians, if your souls were healthful and vigorous, they would perceive incomparably more delight and sweetness in the believing, joyful thoughts of your future blessedness than the soundest stomach finds in its food, or the strongest senses in the enjoyment of their objects; so little painful would this work be to you. But because I know, while we have flesh about us and any remains of that "carnal mind which is enmity against God" and this noble work, that all motives are little enough, I will here lay down some considerations, which, if you will deliberately weigh with an impartial judgment, I doubt not will prove effectual with your hearts, and make you resolve on this excellent duty. More particularly consider, it will evidence your sincere piety; it is the highest excellence of the Christian temper; it is the way to live most comfortably; it will be the best preservative from temptations to sin; it will enliven your graces and duties; it will be your best cordial in all afflictions; it will render you most profitable to others; it will honor God; without it you will disobey the commands and lose the most gracious and delightful discoveries of the word of God: it is also the more reasonable to have your hearts with God, as his is so much on you; and in heaven, where you have so much interest and relation; besides, there is nothing but heaven worth setting your hearts upon.

1. Consider that a heart set upon heaven will be one of the most unquestionable evidences of your sincerity, and a clear discovery of a true work of saving grace upon your souls. You are often asking, "How shall we know that we are truly sanctified?" Here you have a sign infallible from the mouth of Jesus Christ himself: "Where your treasure is, there will your hearts be also." God is the saints' treasure and happiness; heaven is the place where they must fully enjoy him. A heart, therefore, set upon heaven is a heart set upon God; and surely a heart set upon God, through Christ, is the truest evidence of saving grace. When learning will be no proof of grace; when knowledge, duties, gifts will fail; when arguments from thy tongue or hand may be confuted; yet then will this, from the bent of thy heart, prove thee sincere. Take a poor Christian, of a weak understanding, a feeble memory, a stammering tongue; yet his heart is set on God, he hath chosen him for his portion, his thoughts are on eternity, his desires are there; he cries out, "O that I were there!" He takes that day for a time of imprisonment, in which he hath not had one refreshing view of eternity. I had rather die in this man's condition, than in the case of him who hath the most eminent gifts, and is most admired for his performances, while his heart is not

thus taken up with God. The man that Christ will find out at the last day, and condemn for want of a "wedding garment," will be one that wants this frame of heart. The question will not then be, How much have you known, or profest, or talked? but, How much have you loved, and where was your heart? Christians, as you would have a proof of your title to glory, labor to get your hearts above. If sin and Satan keep not your affections from thence, they will never be able to keep away your persons.

2. A heart in heaven is the highest excellence of Christian temper. As there is a common excellence by which Christians differ from the world, so there is this peculiar dignity of spirit, by which the more excellent differ from the rest. As the noblest of creatures, so the noblest of Christians are they whose faces are set most direct for heaven. Such a heavenly saint, who hath been rapt up to God in his contemplations and is newly come down from the views of Christ, what discoveries will he make of those superior regions! how high and sacred is his discourse! enough to convince an understanding hearer that he hath seen the Lord, and that no man could speak such words, except he had been with God. This, this is the noble Christian. The most famous mountains and trees are those that reach near-

est to heaven; and he is the choicest Christian whose heart is most frequently and most delightfully there. If a man have lived near the King, or have seen the Sultan of Persia, or the grand Turk, he will be thought a step higher than his neighbors. What, then, shall we judge of him that daily travels as far as heaven, and there hath seen the King of Kings, hath frequent admittance into the divine presence, and feasteth his soul upon the tree of life? For my part, I value this man before the noblest, the richest, the most learned in the world.

3. A heavenly mind is the nearest and truest way to a life of comfort. The countries far north are cold and frozen, because they are distant from the sun. What makes such frozen, uncomfortable Christians, but their living so far from heaven? And what makes others so warm in comforts, but their living higher, and having nearer access to God? When the sun in the spring draws nearer to our part of the earth, how do all things congratulate its approach! The earth looks green, the trees shoot forth, the plants revive, the birds sing, and all things smile upon us. If we would but try this life with God, and keep these hearts above, what a spring of joy would be within us! How should we forget our winter sorrows? How early should we rise to sing the

praise of our great Creator! O Christian, get above! Those that have been there have found it warmer; and I doubt not but thou hast sometimes tried it thyself. When hast thou largest comforts? Is it not when thou hast conversed with God, and talked with the inhabitants of the higher world, and viewed their mansions, and filled thy soul with the forethoughts of glory? If thou knowest by experience what this practise is, I dare say thou knowest what spiritual joy is. If, as David professes, "the light of God's countenance more gladdens the heart than corn and wine," then, surely, they that draw nearest, and most behold it, must be fullest of these joys. Whom should we blame, then, that we are so void of consolation, but our own negligent hearts? God hath provided us a crown of glory, and promised to set it shortly on our heads, and we will not so much as think of it. He bids us behold and rejoice, and we will not so much as look at it: and yet we complain for want of comfort. It is by believing that we are "filled with joy and peace," and no longer than we continue believing. It is in hope the saints rejoice, and no longer than they continue hoping. God's Spirit worketh our comforts by setting our own spirits at work upon the promises, and raising our thoughts to the place of our comforts. As you would delight a covetous man by showing him gold, so God delights his people by leading them, as it were, into heaven, and showing them himself and their rest with him. He does not kindle our joys while we are idle, or taken up with other things. He gives the fruits of the earth while we plow, and sow, and weed, and water, and dress, and with patience expect his blessing; so doth he give the joys of the soul. I entreat thee, reader, in the name of the Lord, and as thou valuest the life of constant joy and that good conscience which is a continual feast, to enter upon this work seriously, and learn the art of heavenly-mindedness, and thou shalt find the increase a hundredfold, and the benefit abundantly exceed thy labor. But this is the misery of man's nature: tho every man naturally hates sorrow and loves the most merry and joyful life, yet few love the way to joy or will endure the pains by which it is obtained; they will take the first that comes to hand and content themselves with earthly pleasures, rather than ascend to heaven to seek it; and yet, when all is done, they must have it there or be without it.

4. A heart in heaven will be a most excellent preservative against temptations to sin. It will keep the heart well employed. When we are idle, we tempt the devil to tempt us; as careless persons make thieves. A heart in

heaven can reply to the tempter, as Nehemiah did: "I am doing a great work, so that I can not come." It hath no leisure to be lustful or wanton, ambitious or worldly. If you were but busy in your lawful callings, you would not be so ready to hearken to temptations; much less if you were also busy above with God. Would a judge be persuaded to rise from the bench, when he is sitting upon a case of life and death, to go and play with children in the streets? No more will a Christian, when he is taking a survey of his eternal rest, give ear to the alluring charms of Satan. The children of that kingdom should never have time for trifles, especially when they are employed in the affairs of the kingdom; and this employment is one of the saints' chief preservatives from temptations.

A heavenly mind is the freest from sin, because it has truer and livelier apprehensions of spiritual things. He hath so deep an insight into the evil of sin, the vanity of the creature, the brutishness of fleshly, sensual delights, that temptations have little power over him. "In vain the net is spread," says Solomon, "in the sight of any bird." And usually in vain doth Satan lay his snares to entrap the soul that plainly sees them. Earth is the place for his temptations, and the ordinary bait: and how shall these ensnare the

Christian who hath left the earth and walks with God? Is converse with wise and learned men the way to make one wise? Much more is converse with God. If travelers return home with wisdom and experience, how much more he that travels to heaven! If our bodies are suited to the air and climate we most live in, his understanding must be fuller of light who lives with the Father of lights. The men of the world that dwell below, and know no other conversation but earthly, no wonder if their "understanding be darkened," and Satan "take them captive at his will." How can worms and moles see, whose dwelling is always in the earth? While this dust is in their eyes, no wonder they mistake gain for godliness, sin for grace, the world for God, their own wills for the law of Christ, and, in the issue, hell for heaven. But when a Christian withdraws himself from his worldly thoughts and begins to converse with God in heaven, methinks he is, as Nebuchadnezzar, taken from the beasts of the field to the throne, and "his reason returneth unto him." When he has had a glimpse of eternity and looks down on the world again, how doth he charge with folly his neglects of Christ, his fleshly pleasures, his earthly cares! How doth he say of his laughter, It is mad; and of his vain mirth, What doeth it? How doth he verily think there is no man in Bedlam so truly mad as wilful sinners, and unworthy slighters of Christ and glory! This makes a dying man usually wiser than others, because he looks on eternity as near, and hath more heart-piercing thoughts of it than he ever had in health and prosperity. Then many of the most bitter enemies of the saints have their eyes opened, and like Balaam, cry out, "O that I might die the death of the righteous, and that my last end might be like this!" Yet let the same men recover, and lose their apprehensions of the life to come, and how quickly do they lose their understanding with it! Tell a dying sinner of the riches, honors, or pleasures of the world, and would he not answer, "What is all this to me, who must presently appear before God and give an account of all my life?" Christian, if the apprehended nearness of eternity will work such strange effects upon the ungodly, and make them so much wiser than before, O what rare effects would it produce in thee, couldst thou always dwell in the views of God, and in lively thoughts of thy everlasting state! Surely a believer, if he improve his faith, may ordinarily have more quickening apprehensions of the life to come, in the time of his health, than an unbeliever hath at the hour of his death.

A heavenly mind is also fortified against

temptations, because the affections are thoroughly prepossest with the high delights of another world. He that loves most, and not he that only knows most, will most easily resist the motions of sin. The will doth as sweetly relish goodness as the understanding doth truth; and here lies much of a Christian's strength. When thou hast had a fresh, delightful taste of heaven, thou wilt not be so easily persuaded from it. You can not persuade a child to part with his sweetmeats while the taste is in his mouth. O that you would be much in feeding on the hidden manna, and frequently tasting the delights of heaven! How would this confirm thy resolutions, and make thee despise the fooleries of the world, and scorn to be cheated with such childish toys. If the devil had set upon Peter in the mount of transfiguration, when he saw Moses and Elias talking with Christ, would he so easily have been drawn to deny his Lord? What! with all that glory in his eye? No. So if he should set upon a believing soul when he is taken up into the mount with Christ, what should such a soul say? "Get thee behind me, Satan; wouldst thou persuade me hence with trifling pleasures, and steal my heart from this my rest? Wouldst thou have me sell these joys for nothing? Is any honor or delight like this? or can that be profit, for which I must lose this?'' But Satan stays till we are come down, and the taste of heaven is out of our mouths, and the glory we saw is even forgotten, and then he easily deceives our hearts. Tho the Israelites below eat and drink and rise up to play before their idol, Moses in the mount will not do so. O, if we could keep the taste of our souls continually delighted with the sweetness above, with what disdain should we spit out the baits of sin!

Besides, while the heart is set on heaven, a man is under God's protection. If Satan then assault us, God is more engaged for our defense, and will doubtless stand by us and say, ''My grace is sufficient for thee.'' When a man is in the way of God's blessing, he is in the less danger of sin's enticing. Amidst thy temptations, Christian reader, use much this powerful remedy; keep close with God by a heavenly mind; follow your business above with Christ, and you will find this a surer help than any other. ''The way of life is above to the wise, that he may depart from hell beneath.'' Remember that ''Noah was a just man, and perfect in his generation''; for he ''walked with God''; and that God said to Abraham, ''Walk before me, and be thou perfect.''

5. The diligent keeping your hearts in heav-

en will maintain the vigor of all your graces, and put life into all your duties. The heavenly Christian is the lively Christian. It is our strangeness to heaven that makes us so dull. How will the soldier hazard his life, and the mariner pass through storms and waves, and no difficulty keep them back, when they think of an uncertain, perishing treasure! What life, then, would it put into a Christian's endeavors, if he would frequently think of his everlasting treasure! We run so slowly, and strive so lazily, because we so little mind the prize. Observe but the man who is much in heaven, and you shall see he is not like other Christians; something of what he hath seen above appeareth in all his duty and conversation. If a preacher, how heavenly are his sermons! If a private Christian, what heavenly converse, prayers, and deportment! Set yourself upon this employment, and others will see the face of your conversation shine, and say, Surely he hath been "with God on the mount." But if you lie, complaining of deadness and dulness; that you can not love Christ, nor rejoice in his love; that you have no life in prayer, or any other duty, and yet neglect this quickening employment; you are the cause of your own complaints. Is not thy life "hid with Christ in God?" Where must thou go but to Christ for it? And where is that, but to heaven, "where Christ is?" "Thou wilt not come to Christ, that thou mayest have life." If thou wouldst have light and heat, why art thou no more in the sunshine? For want of this recourse to heaven, thy soul is as a lamp not lighted, and thy duties as a sacrifice without fire. Fetch one coal daily from this altar, and see if thy offering will not burn. Light thy lamp at this flame, and feed it daily with oil from hence, and see if it will not gloriously shine. Keep close to this reviving fire, and see if thy affections will not be warm. In thy want of love to God, lift up thy eye of faith to heaven, behold his beauty, contemplate his excellencies, and see whether his amiableness and perfect goodness will not ravish thy heart. As exercise gives appetite, strength, and vigor to the body, so these heavenly exercises will quickly cause the increase of grace and spiritual life.

Besides, it is not false or strange fire which you fetch from heaven for your sacrifices: the zeal which is kindled by your meditations on heaven is most likely to be a heavenly zeal. Some men's fervency is only drawn from their books, some from the sharpness of affliction, some from the mouth of a moving minister, and some from the attention of an auditory; but he that knows this way to heaven and derives it daily from the true fountain, shall have his soul revived with the water of life, and enjoy that quickening which is peculiar to the saints. By this faith thou mayest offer Abel's sacrifice, more excellent than that of common men, and "by it obtain witness that thou art righteous, God testifying of thy gifts" that they are sincere. When others are ready, like Baal's priests, to "cut themselves" because their sacrifice will not burn, thou mayst breathe the spirit of Elijah, and in the chariot of contemplation soar aloft till thy soul and sacrifice gloriously flame, tho the flesh and the world should cast upon them all the water of their opposing enmity. Say not, How can mortals ascend to heaven? Faith hath wings, and meditation is its chariot. Faith is as a burning glass to thy sacrifice, and meditation sets it to the face of the sun; only take it not away too soon, but hold it there awhile, and thy soul will feel the happy effect. Reader, art thou not thinking, when thou seest a lively Christian and hearest his fervent prayers and edifying discourse, "O how happy a man is this! O that my soul were in this blessed condition!" Why, I here advise thee from God, set thy soul conscientiously to this work, wash thee frequently in this Jordan, and thy leprous, dead soul will revive, "and thou shalt know that there is a God in Israel,'' and that thou mayst live a vigorous and joyful life, if thou dost not wilfully neglect thy own mercies.

6. Frequent believing views of glory are the most precious cordials in all afflictions. These cordials, by cheering our spirits, render our sufferings far more easy, enable us to bear them with patience and joy, and so strengthen our resolutions that we forsake not Christ for fear of trouble. If the way be ever so rough, can it be tedious, if it lead to heaven? O sweet sickness, reproaches, imprisonments, or death, accompanied with these tastes of our future rest! This keeps the suffering from the soul, so that it can only touch the flesh. Had it not been for that little (alas! too little) taste which I had of rest, my sufferings would have been grievous, and death more terrible. I may say, "I had fainted, unless I had believed to see the goodness of the Lord in the land of the living." Unless this promised rest "had been my delight, I should then have perished in mine affliction. One thing have I desired of the Lord, that will I seek after; that I may dwell in the house of the Lord all the days of my life, to behold the beauty of the Lord, and to inquire in his temple. For in the time of trouble he shall hide me in his pavilion; in the secret of his tabernacle shall he hide me; he shall set me

upon a rock. And now shall mine head be lifted up above mine enemies round about me. Therefore will I offer in his tabernacle sacrifices of joy; I will sing, yea, I will sing praises unto the Lord." All sufferings are nothing to us, so far as we have these supporting joys. When persecution and fear have shut the doors, Christ can come in, and stand in the midst, and say to his disciples, "Peace be unto you." Paul and Silas can be in heaven, even when they are thrust into the inner prison, their bodies scourged with "many stripes, and their feet fast in the stocks." The martyrs find more rest in their flames than their persecutors in their pomp and tyranny; because they foresee the flames they escape, and the rest to which their fiery chariot is conveying them. If the Son of God will walk with us, we are safe in the midst of those flames which shall devour them that cast us in. Abraham went out of his country, "not knowing whither he went;" because "he looked for a city which hath foundations, whose builder and maker is God." Moses "esteemed the reproach of Christ greater riches than the treasures in Egypt; because he had respect unto the recompense of reward. He forsook Egypt, not fearing the wrath of the king; because he endured as seeing him who is invisible. Others were tortured, not accepting deliverance, that they might obtain a better resurrection." Even Jesus, "the author and finisher of our faith, for the joy that was set before him, endured the cross, despising the shame, and is set down at the right hand of the throne of God."

This is the noble advantage of faith: it can look on the means and end together. The great reason of our impatience and censuring of God, is that we gaze on the evil itself, but fix not our thoughts on what is beyond it. They that saw Christ only on the cross or in the grave shook their heads and thought him lost; but God saw him dying, buried, rising, glorified; and all this at one view. Faith will in this imitate God, so far as it hath the glass of a promise to help it. We see God burying us under ground, but we foresee not the spring, when we shall all revive. Could we but clearly see heaven as the end of all God's dealings with us, surely none of his dealings could be grievous. If God would once raise us to this life, we should find, that tho heaven and sin are at a great distance, yet heaven and a prison or banishment, heaven and the belly of a whale or a den of lions; heaven and consuming sickness or invading death, are at no such distance. But as "Abraham saw Christ's day and rejoiced," so we, in our most forlorn state, might see that day when Christ

shall give us rest, and therein rejoice. I beseech thee, Christian, for the honor of the
gospel, and for thy soul's comfort, leave not
this heavenly art to be learned when, in thy
greatest extremity, thou hast most need to use
it. He that, with Stephen, "sees the glory of
God, and Jesus standing on the right hand of
God," will comfortably bear the shower of
stones. "The joy of the Lord is our strength,"
and that joy must be drawn from the place of
our joy; and if we walk without our strength,
how long are we likely to endure?

7. He whose conversation is in heaven, is
the profitable Christian to all about him.
When a man is in a strange country, how
glad is he of the company of one of his own
nation! how delightful is it to talk of their
own country, their acquaintance, and affairs
at home! With what pleasure did Joseph
talk with his brethren, and inquire after his
father and his brother Benjamin! Is it not
so to a Christian, to talk with his brethren that
have been above, and inquire after his Father,
and Christ his Lord? When a worldly man
will talk of nothing but the world, and a poli-
tician of state affairs, and a mere scholar of
human learning, and a common professor of
his duties; the heavenly man will be speaking
of heaven, and the strange glory his faith hath
seen, and our speedy and blessed meeting

there. O how refreshing and useful are his expressions! How his words pierce and melt the heart and transform the hearers into other men! How doth his "doctrine drop as the rain, and his speech distil as the dew, as the small rain upon the tender herb, and as the showers upon the grass," while his lips publish the name of the Lord, and ascribe greatness unto his God! His sweet discourse of heaven is like the "box of precious ointment," which, being "poured upon the head of Christ, filled the house with the odor." All that are near may be refreshed by it.

Happy the people that have a heavenly minister! Happy the children and servants that have a heavenly father or master! Happy the man that hath a heavenly companion, who will watch over thy ways, strengthen thee when thou art weak, cheer thee when thou art drooping, and "comfort thee with the comfort wherewith he himself" hath been so often comforted of God! This is he that will always be blowing at the spark of thy spiritual life and drawing thy soul to God, and will say to thee, as the Samaritan woman, "Come and see one that hath told me all that ever I did"; one that hath loved our souls to the death. "Is not this the Christ?" Is not "the knowledge of God and him eternal life?" Is it not the glory of the saints to see his glory? Come to this man's house and sit at his table, and he will feast thy soul with the dainties of heaven; travel with him by the way, and he will direct and quicken thee in thy journey to heaven; trade with him in the world, and he will counsel thee to buy "the pearl of great price." If thou wrong him, he can pardon thee, remembering that Christ hath pardoned his greater offenses. If thou be angry, he is meek, considering the meekness of his heavenly Pattern; or, if he fall out with you, he is soon reconciled, when he recollects that in heaven you must be everlasting friends. This is the Christian of the right stamp, and all about him are better for him. How unprofitable is the society of all other sorts of Christians in comparison with this! If a man should come from heaven, how would men long to hear what reports he would make of the other world, and what he had seen, and what the blessed there enjoy! Would they not think this man the best companion, and his discourses the most profitable? Why, then, do you value the company of saints no more, and inquire no more of them, and relish their discourse no better? For every saint shall go to heaven in person, and is frequently there in spirit, and hath often viewed it in the glass of the gospel. For my part, I had

rather have the company of a heavenly-
minded Christian than that of the most
learned disputants or princely commanders.

8. No man so highly honoreth God as he
whose conversation is in heaven. Is not a
parent dishonored when his children feed
on husks, are clothed in rags, and keep company with none but rogues and beggars? And
is not our heavenly Father, when we, who
call ourselves his children, feed on earth,
and the garb of our souls is like that of the
world, and our hearts familiarly converse with
and "cleave to the dust," rather than stand
continually in our Father's presence? Surely
we live below the children of the King not according to the height of our hopes, nor the
provision of our Father's house, and the
great preparations made for his saints. It is
well we have a Father of tender compassion,
who will own his children in rags. If he did
not first challenge his interest in us, neither
ourselves nor others could know us to be his
people. But when a Christian can live above,
and rejoice his soul with the things that are
unseen, how is God honored by such a one!
The Lord will testify for him: This man believes me, and takes me at my word, he rejoices in my promise before he has possession;
he can be thankful for what his bodily eyes
never saw: his rejoicing is not in the flesh:

his heart is with me; he loves my presence, and he shall surely enjoy it in my kingdom for ever. "Blessed are they that have not seen, and yet have believed. Them that honor me, I will honor." How did God esteem himself honored by Caleb and Joshua when they went into the promised land and brought back to their brethren a taste of the fruits, and spake well of the good land, and encouraged the people! What a promise and recompense did they receive!

9. A soul that does not set its affections on things above disobeys the commands and loses the most gracious and delightful discoveries of the word of God. The same God that hath commanded thee to believe and to be a Christian hath commanded to "seek those things which are above, where Christ sitteth on the right hand of God: and to set our affections on things above, not on things on the earth." The same God that has forbidden thee to murder, steal, or commit adultery, has forbidden thee the neglect of this great duty; and darest thou wilfully disobey him? Why not make conscience of one as well as the other? He hath made it thy duty, as well as the means of thy comfort, that a double bond may engage thee not to forsake thy own mercies. Besides, what are all the most glorious descriptions of heaven, all those discover-

ies of our future blessedness and precious
promises of our rest, but lost to thee? Are
not these the stars in the firmament of Scripture, and the golden lines in that book of God?
Methinks thou shouldst not part with one of
these promises, no, not for a world. As heav-
en is the perfection of all our mercies, so
the promises of it in the gospel are the very
soul of the gospel. Is a comfortable word
from the mouth of God of such worth that all
the comforts in the world are nothing to it?
And dost thou neglect and overlook so many
of them? Why should God reveal so much
of his counsel, and tell us beforehand of the
joys we shall possess, but to make us know
it for our joy? If it had not been to fill us
with the delights of our foreknown blessedness, he might have kept his purpose to himself, and never have let us know it till we
came to enjoy it. Yea, when we had got
possession of our rest, he might still have con-
cealed its eternity from us, and then the fears
of losing it would have diminished the sweetness of our joys. But it hath pleased our
Father to open his counsel, and let us know
the very intent of his heart, that our joy
might be full, and that we might live as the
heirs of such a kingdom. And shall we now
overlook all? Shall we live in earthly cares
and sorrows, and rejoice no more in these

discoveries than if the Lord had never written them? If thy prince had but sealed thee a patent of some lordship, how oft wouldst thou cast thy eyes upon it and make it thy delightful study, till thou shouldst come to possess the dignity itself! And hath God sealed thee a patent of heaven, and dost thou let it lie by thee as if thou hadst forgot it? O that our hearts were as high as our hopes, and our hopes as high as these infallible promises!

10. It is but equal that our hearts should be on God, when the heart of God is so much on us. If the Lord of glory can stoop so low as to set his heart on sinful dust, methinks we should easily be persuaded to set our hearts on Christ and glory, and ascend to him in our daily affections, who so much condescends to us. Christian, dost thou not perceive that the heart of God is set upon thee, and that he is still minding thee with tender love, even when thou forgettest both thyself and him? Is he not following thee with daily mercies, moving upon thy soul, providing for thy body, preserving both? Doth he not bear thee continually in the arms of love, and promise that "all shall work together for thy good," and suit all his dealings to thy greatest advantage, and "give his angels charge over thee?" And canst thou be taken up with the joys below and forget thy Lord, who forgets

not thee? Unkind ingratitude! When he speaks of his own kindness for us, hear what he says: "Zion said, The Lord hath forsaken me, and my Lord hath forgotten me. Can a woman forget her sucking child, that she should not have compassion on the son of her womb? Yea, they may forget, yet will I not forget thee. Behold, I have graven thee upon the palms of my hands; thy walls are continually before me." But when he speaks of our regards to him, the case is otherwise. "Can a maid forget her ornaments, or a bride her attire? Yet my people have forgotten me, days without number." As if he should say, "You will not rise one morning but you will remember to cover your nakedness, nor forget your vanity of dress; and are these of more worth than your God? of more importance than your eternal life? And yet you can forget these, day after day." Give not God cause thus to expostulate with us. Rather let our souls get up to God, and visit him every morning, and our hearts be toward him every moment.

11. Our interest in heaven, and our relation to it, should continually keep our hearts upon it. There our Father keeps his court. We call him "Our Father, who art in heaven." Unworthy children, that can be so taken up in their play as to be mindless of

such a Father. There also is Christ, our head, our husband, our life; and shall we not look toward him, and send to him as oft as we can, till we come to see him face to face? Since "the heavens must receive him until the times of the restitution of all things," let them also receive our hearts with him. There also is the "New Jerusalem, which is the mother of us all." And there are multitudes of our elder brethren. There are our friends and old acquaintance, whose society in the flesh we so much delighted in, and whose departure hence we so much lamented; and is this not attractive to thy thoughts? If they were within thy reach on earth, thou wouldst go and visit them; and why not oftener visit them in spirit, and rejoice beforehand to think of meeting them there? "Socrates rejoiced that he should die, because he believed he should see Homer, Hesiod, and other eminent persons. How much more do I rejoice," said a pious old minister, "who am sure to see Christ my Savior, the eternal Son of God, in his assumed flesh; besides so many wise, holy, and renowned patriarchs, prophets, and apostles." A believer should look to heaven, and contemplate the blessed state of the saints, and think with himself, "Tho I am not yet so happy as to be with you, yet this is my daily comfort—you are my brethren and fellow-members in Christ, and therefore your joys are my joys, and your glory, by this near relation, is my glory; especially while I believe in the same Christ, and hold fast the same faith and obedience by which you were thus dignified, and rejoice in spirit with you, and congratulate your happiness in my daily meditations.''

Moreover, our house and home is above, ''For we know that if our earthly house of this tabernacle were dissolved, we have a building of God, a house not made with hands, eternal in the heavens.'' Why do we then look no oftener toward it, and ''groan, earnestly desiring to be clothed upon with our house which is from heaven?'' If our home were far meaner, surely we should remember it, because it is our home. If you were but banished into a strange land, how frequently would your thoughts be at home! And why is it not thus with us in respect to heaven? Is not that more truly and properly our home where we must take up our everlasting abode, than this, which we are every hour expecting to be separated from and to see no more? We are strangers, and that is our country. We are heirs, and that is our inheritance; even ''an inheritance incorruptible, undefiled, and that fadeth not away, reserved in heaven for us.'' We are here in continual distress

and want, and there lies our substance; even
"a better and an enduring substance." Yea,
the very hope of our souls is there; all our
hope of relief from our distresses; all our
hope of happiness, when here we are miserable; all this "hope is laid up for us in heaven." Why, beloved Christians, have we so
much interest and so few thoughts there? so
near relation and so little affection? Doth it
become us to be delighted in the company of
strangers, so as to forget our Father and our
Lord? or to be so well pleased with those
that hate and grieve us as to forget our best
and dearest friends; or to be so fond of borrowed trifles as to forget our own possession
and treasure? or to be so much imprest with
fears and wants as to forget our eternal joy
and rest? God usually pleads his property
in us; and thence concludes he will do us
good, even because we are his own people, whom
he hath chosen out of all the world. Why
then do we not plead our interest in him, and
so raise our hearts above; even because he is
our own God, and because the place is our
own possession? Men commonly overlove and
overvalue their own things, and mind them
too much. O that we could mind our own
inheritance and value it half as much as it
deserves.

12. Once more consider, there is nothing

but heaven worth setting our hearts upon. If
God have them not, who shall? If thou mind
not thy rest, what wilt thou mind? Hast
thou found out some other god; or something
that will serve thee instead of rest? Hast
thou found on earth an eternal happiness?
Where is it? What is it made of? Who was
the man that found it out? Who was he that
last enjoyed it? Where dwelt he? What was
his name? Or art thou the first that ever
discovered heaven on earth? Ah, wretch!
trust not to thy discoveries; boast not of thy
gain till experience bid thee boast. Disquiet
not thyself in looking for that which is not
on earth, lest thou learn thy experience with
the loss of thy soul, which thou mightest have
learned on easier terms; even by the warn-
ings of God in his word, and the loss of thousands of souls before thee. If Satan should
take thee up to the mountain of temptation,
and "show thee all the kingdoms of the
world, and the glory of them," he could show
thee nothing that is worthy thy thoughts,
much less to be preferred before thy rest.
Indeed, so far as duty and necessity require
it, we must be content to mind the things below; but who is he that contains himself within the compass of those limits? and yet, if
we ever so diligently contract our cares and
thoughts, we shall find the least to be bitter

and burdensome. Christian, see the emptiness
of all these things, and the preciousness of the
things above. If thy thoughts should, like
the laborious bee, go over the world from
flower to flower, from creature to creature,
they would bring no honey or sweetness home
save what they gathered from their relations
to eternity. Tho every truth of God is precious and ought to be defended, yet even all
our study of truth should be still in reference
to our rest; for the observation is too true,
"that the lovers of controversies in religion
have never been warmed with one spark of the
love of God." And as for minding the "affairs of the Church and the State," so far as
they illustrate the providence of God and tend
to the settling of the gospel and the government of Christ, and consequently to the saving of our own souls and those of our pos-
terity, they are well worth our diligent observation; but these are only their relations to
eternity. Even all our dealings in the world,
our buying and selling, our eating and drink-
ing, our building and marrying, our peace
and war, so far as they relate not to the life
to come, but tend only to the pleasing of the
flesh, are not worthy the frequent thoughts
of a Christian. And now, doth not thy conscience say that there is nothing but heaven,
and the way to it, that is worth thy minding?

Now, reader, are these considerations weighty or not? Have I proved it to be thy duty to keep thy heart on things above, or have I not? If thou say, Not, I am confident thou contradictest thy own conscience. If thou acknowledge thyself convinced of the duty, that very tongue of thine shall condemn thee, and that confession be pleaded against thee, if thou wilfully neglect such a confest duty. Be thoroughly willing, and the work is more than half done. I have now a few plain directions to give you for your help in this great work; but, alas! it is in vain to mention them, except you be willing to put them into practise. However, I will propose them to thee, and may the Lord persuade thy heart to the work!

The Nature of Heavenly Contemplation; With the Time, Place, and Temper Fittest for It

Once more I entreat thee, reader, as thou makest conscience of a revealed duty and darest not wilfully resist the Spirit; as thou valuest the high delights of a saint, and the soul-ravishing exercise of heavenly contemplation; that thou diligently study, and speedily and faithfully practise the following directions. If, by this means, thou dost not find an increase of all thy graces, and dost not grow beyond the stature of a common Christian, and art not made more serviceable in thy place, and more precious in the eyes of all discerning persons; if thy soul enjoy not more communion with God, and thy life be not fuller of comfort, and thou hast not more support in a dying hour; then cast away these directions, and exclaim against me forever as a deceiver.

The duty which I press upon thee so earnestly, and in the practise of which I am now to direct thee, is, "The set and solemn acting of all the powers of thy soul in meditation upon the everlasting rest." . . .

It is not improper to illustrate a little the manner in which we have described this duty of meditation, or the considering and contemplating of spiritual things. It is confest to be a duty by all, but practically denied by most. Many that make conscience of other duties easily neglect this. They are troubled if they omit a sermon, a fast, or a prayer, in public or private; yet were never troubled that they have omitted meditation perhaps all their lifetime to this very day; tho it be that duty by which all other duties are improved, and by which the soul digests truth for its nourishment and comfort. It was God's command to Joshua, "This book of the law shall not depart out of thy mouth, but thou shalt meditate therein day and night, that thou mayest observe to do according to all that is written therein." As digestion turns food into chyle and blood for vigorous health, so meditation turns the truths received and remembered into warm affection, firm resolution, and holy conversation.

This meditation is the acting of all the powers of the soul. It is the work of the living, and not of the dead. It is a work the most spiritual and sublime, and therefore not to be well performed by a heart that is merely carnal and earthly. Men must necessarily have some relation to heaven before they can familiarly converse there. I suppose them to be such as have a title to rest, when I persuade them to rejoice in the meditations of rest. And supposing thee to be a Christian, I am now exhorting thee to be an active Christian. And it is the work of the soul I am setting thee to, for bodily exercise here profiteth little. And it must have all the powers of the soul to distinguish it from the common meditation of students; for the understanding is not the whole soul, and therefore can not do the whole work. As in the body, the stomach must turn the food into chyle and prepare for the liver, the liver and spleen turn it into

blood and prepare for the heart and brain;
so in the soul the understanding must take
in truths and prepare them for the will, and
that for the affections. Christ and heaven
have various excellencies, and therefore God
hath formed the soul with different powers
for apprehending these excellencies. What
the better had we been for odoriferous flowers
if we had no smell? or what good would
language or music have done us if we could
not hear? or what pleasure should we have
found in meats and drinks without the sense
of taste? So what good could all the glory
of heaven have done us, or what pleasure
should we have had in the perfection of God
himself, if we had been without the affections of love and joy? And what strength or
sweetness canst thou possibly receive by thy
meditations on eternity, while thou dost not
exercise those affections of the soul by which
thou must be sensible of this sweetness and
strength? It is the mistake of Christians to
think that meditation is only the work of the
understanding and memory, when every
schoolboy can do this, or persons that hate
the things which they think on. So that you
see there is more to be done than barely to
remember and think of heaven. As some
labors not only stir a hand or a foot, but
exercise the whole body, so doth meditation

the whole soul. As the affections of sinners are set on the world, are turned to idols and fallen from God as well as their understanding; so must their affections be reduced to God as well as the understanding; and as their whole soul was filled with sin before, so the whole must be filled with God now. See David's description of the blessed man: "His delight is in the law of the Lord, and in his law doth he meditate day and night."

This meditation is set and solemn. As there is solemn prayer, when we set ourselves wholly to that duty; and ejaculatory prayer, when, in the midst of other business, we send up some short request to God; so also there is solemn meditation, when we apply ourselves wholly to that work; and transient meditation, when, in the midst of other business, we have some good thoughts of God in our minds. And as solemn prayer is either set in a constant course of duty, or occasional, at an extraordinary season; so also is meditation. Now, tho I would persuade you to that meditation which is mixt with your common labors, and also that to which special occasions direct you; yet I would have you likewise make it a constant standing duty, as you do hearing, praying, and reading the Scriptures; and no more intermix other matters with it, than you would with prayer, or other stated solemnities.

This meditation is upon thy everlasting rest. I would not have you cast off your other meditations; but surely, as heaven hath the preeminence in perfection, it should have it also in our meditation. That which will make us most happy when we possess it will make us most joyful when we meditate upon it. Other meditations are as numerous as there are lines in the Scripture, or creatures in the universe, or particular providences in the government of the world. But this is a walk to Mount Sion; from the kingdoms of this world to the kingdom of saints; from earth to heaven; from time to eternity: it is walking upon sun, moon and stars, in the garden and paradise of God. It may seem far off; but spirits are quick: whether in the body or out of the body, their motion is swift. You need not fear, like the men of the world, lest these thoughts should make you mad. It is in heaven, and not hell, that I persuade you to walk. It is joy, and not sorrow, that I persuade you to exercise. I urge you to look on no deformed objects, but only upon the ravishing glory of saints, and the unspeakable excellencies of the God of glory, and the beams that stream from the face of his Son. Will it distract a man to think of his only happiness? Will it distract the miserable to think of mercy, or the prisoner to foresee deliverance, or the poor to

think of approaching riches and honor? Methinks it should rather make a man mad to
think of living in a world of wo, and abiding
in poverty and sickness among the rage of
wicked men, than to think of living with
Christ in bliss. "But wisdom is justified of
all her children." Knowledge hath no enemy
but the ignorant. This heavenly course was
never spoken against by any but those that
never knew it or never used it. I fear more
the neglect of men that approve it, than the
opposition or arguments of any against it.

First. As to the fittest time for this heavenly contemplation, let me only advise that it be
stated—frequent—and seasonable.

1. Give it a stated time. If thou suit thy
time to the advantage of the work, without
placing any religion in the time itself, thou
hast no need to fear superstition. Stated time
is a hedge to duty, and defends it against
many temptations to omission. Some have not
their time at command, and therefore can not
set their hours; and many are so poor that
the necessities of their families deny them
this freedom; such persons should be watchful to redeem time as much as they can, and
take their vacant opportunities as they fall,
and especially join meditation and prayer as
much as they can with the labors of their
calling. Yet those who have more time to

spare from their worldly necessities, and are masters of their time, I still advise to keep this duty to a stated time. And indeed, if every work of the day had its appointed time, we should be better skilled both in redeeming time and performing duty.

2. Let it be frequent as well as stated. How oft it should be I can not determine, because men's circumstances differ; but in general, Scripture requires it to be frequent, when it mentions meditating day and night. For those, therefore, who can conveniently omit other business, I advise that it be once a day at least.

Frequency in heavenly contemplation is particularly important to prevent a shyness between God and thy soul. Frequent society breeds familiarity, and familiarity increases love and delight, and makes us bold in our addresses. The chief end of this duty is to have acquaintance and fellowship with God; and therefore, if thou come but seldom to it, thou wilt still keep thyself a stranger. When a man feels his need of God, and must seek his help in a time of necessity, then it is great encouragement to go to a God we know and are acquainted with. "O," saith the heavenly Christian, "I know both whither I go, and to whom. I have gone this way many a time before now. It is the same God that I daily converse with, and the way has been my daily walk. God knows me well enough, and I have some knowledge of him." On the other hand, what a horror and discouragement will it be to the soul, when it is forced to fly to God in straits, to think, "Alas! I know not whither to go. I never went the way before. I have no acquaintance at the court of heaven. My soul knows not that God that I must speak to, and I fear he will not know my soul." But especially when we come to die, and must immediately appear before this God, and expect to enter into his eternal rest, then the difference will plainly appear; then what a joy will it be to think, "I am going to the place that I daily conversed in; to the place from whence I tasted such frequent delights; to that God whom I have met in my meditation so often! My heart hath been in heaven before now, and hath often tasted its reviving sweetness; and if my eyes were so enlightened and my spirits so refreshed when I had but a taste, what will it be when I shall feed on it freely?" On the contrary, what a terror will it be to think, "I must die and go I know not whither; from a place where I am acquainted to a place where I have no familiarity or knowledge!" It is an inexpressible horror to a dying man to have strange thoughts of God and heaven.

I am persuaded that it is the neglect of this duty which so commonly makes death, even to godly men, unwelcome and uncomfortable. Therefore I persuade to frequency in this duty.

And as it will prevent shyness between thee and God, so also it will prevent unskilfulness in the duty itself. How awkwardly do men set their hands to a work in which they are seldom employed! Whereas frequency will habituate thy heart to the work, and make it more easy and delightful. The hill which made thee pant and blow at first going up, thou mayest easily run up when thou art once accustomed to it.

Thou wilt also prevent the loss of the heat and life thou hast obtained. If thou eat but once in two or three days, thou wilt lose thy strength as fast as it comes. If in holy meditation thou get near to Christ and warm thy heart with the fire of love, and then come but seldom, thy former coldness will soon return; especially as the work is so spiritual and against the bent of depraved nature. It is true, the intermixing of other duties, especially secret prayer, may do much to the keeping of thy heart above; but meditation is the life of most other duties, and the view of heaven is the life of meditation.

3. Choose also the most seasonable time.

All things are beautiful and excellent in their season. Unseasonableness may lose the fruit of thy labor, may raise difficulties in the work, and may turn a duty to a sin. The same hour may be seasonable to one and unseasonable to another. Servants and laborers must take that season which their business can best afford; either while at work, or in traveling, or when they lie awake in the night. Such as can choose what time of the day they will, should observe when they find their spirits most active and fit for contemplation, and fix upon that as the stated time. I have always found that the fittest time for myself is the evening, from sun-setting to the twilight. I the rather mention this, because it was the experience of a better and wiser man; for it is expressly said, "Isaac went out to meditate in the field at the even-tide."

The Lord's Day is exceeding seasonable for this exercise. When should we more seasonably contemplate our rest than on that day of rest which typifies it to us? It being a day appropriated to spiritual duties, methinks we should never exclude this duty, which is so eminently spiritual. I verily think this is the chief work of a Christian Sabbath, and most agreeable to the design of its positive institution. What fitter time to converse with our Lord than on the Lord's day? What fitter

day to ascend to heaven than that on which
he arose from earth, and fully triumphed over
death and hell? The fittest temper for a true
Christian is, like John, to "be in the Spirit on
the Lord's day." And what can bring us to
this joy in the Spirit but the spiritual beholding of our approaching glory? Take notice
of this, you that spend the Lord's day only
in public worship; your allowing no time to
private duty, and, therefore, neglecting this
spiritual duty of meditation, is very hurtful
to your souls. You, also, that have time on the
Lord's day for idleness and vain discourse,
were you but acquainted with this duty of
contemplation, you would need no other pas-
time; you would think the longest day short
enough, and be sorry that the night had
shortened your pleasure. Christians, let
heaven have more share in your Sabbaths,
where you must shortly keep your everlasting
Sabbaths. Use your Sabbaths as steps to
glory, till you have passed them all, and are
there arrived. Especially you that are poor
and can not take time in the week as you
desire, see that you well improve this day; as
your bodies rest from their labors, let your
spirits seek after rest from God.

Besides the constant seasonableness of every
day and particularly every Lord's day, there

are also more peculiar seasons for heavenly contemplation. As for instance:

When God hath more abundantly warmed thy spirit with fire from above, then thou mayest soar with greater freedom. A little labor will set thy heart a-going at such a time as this, whereas at another time thou mayest take pains to little purpose. Observe the gales of the Spirit, and how the Spirit of Christ doth move thy spirit. "Without Christ we can do nothing"; and therefore let us be doing while he is doing! and be sure not to be out of the way, nor asleep, when he comes. When the Spirit finds thy heart, like Peter, in prison and in irons, and smites thee, and says, "Arise up quickly, and follow me!" be sure thou then arise and follow; and thou shalt find thy chains fall off, and all doors will open, and thou wilt be at heaven before thou art aware.

Another peculiar season for this duty is when thou art in a suffering, distressed, or tempted state. When should we take our cordials but in time of fainting? When is it more seasonable to walk to heaven than when we know not in what corner of earth to live with comfort? Or when should our thoughts converse more above than when we have nothing but grief below? Where should Noah's dove be but in the ark, when the waters cover all the earth and she can not find rest for the sole of her foot? What should we think on but our Father's house, when we have not even the husks of the world to feed upon? Surely God sends thy afflictions for this very purpose. Happy art thou, poor man, if thou make this use of thy poverty! and thou that art sick, if thou so improve thy sickness! It is seasonable to go to the promised land when our burdens are increased in Egypt and our straits in the wilderness! Reader, if thou knewest what a cordial to thy griefs the serious views of glory are, thou wouldst less fear these harmless troubles, and more use that preserving, reviving remedy. "In the multitude of my" troubled "thoughts within me," saith David, "thy comforts delight my soul." "I reckon," saith Paul, "that the sufferings of this present time are not worthy to be compared with the glory which shall be revealed in us." "For which cause we faint not; but tho our outward man perish, yet the inward man is renewed day by day. For our light affliction, which is but for a moment, worketh for us a far more exceeding and eternal weight of glory, while we look not at the things which are seen, but at the things which are not seen; for the things which are seen are temporal, but the things which are not seen are eternal.''

And another season peculiarly fit for this heavenly duty is when the messengers of God summon us to die. When should we more frequently sweeten our souls with the believing thoughts of another life than when we find that this is almost ended? No men have greater need of supporting joys than dying men; and these joys must be drawn from our eternal joy. As heavenly delights are sweetest when nothing earthly is joined with them, so the delights of dying Christians are oftentimes the sweetest they ever had. What a prophetic blessing had dying Isaac and Jacob for their sons! With what a heavenly song and divine benediction did Moses conclude his life? What heavenly advice and prayer had the disciples from their Lord, when he was about to leave them! When Paul was ''ready to be offered,'' what heavenly exhortation and advice did he give the Philippians, Timothy, and the elders of Ephesus! How near to heaven was John in Patmos, but a little before his translation thither! It is the general temper of the saints to be then most heavenly when they are nearest heaven. If it be thy case, reader, to perceive thy dying time draw on, O where should thy heart now be but with Christ? Methinks thou shouldst even behold him standing by thee, and shouldst bespeak him as thy Father, thy Husband, thy Physician, thy Friend. Methinks thou shouldst, as it were, see the angels about thee, waiting to perform their last office to thy soul; even those angels which disdained not to carry into Abraham's bosom the soul of Lazarus, nor will think much to conduct thee thither. Look upon thy pain and sickness as Jacob did on Joseph's chariots, and let thy spirit revive within thee, and say, "It is enough. Christ is yet alive; because he liveth, I shall live also." Dost thou need the choicest cordials? Here are choicer than the world can afford; here are all the joys of heaven, even the vision of God and Christ, and whatever the blessed here possess. These dainties are offered thee by the hand of Christ; he hath written the receipt in the promises of the gospel; he hath prepared the ingredients in heaven; only put forth the hand of faith and feed upon them, and rejoice, and live. The Lord saith to thee, as to Elijah, "Arise and eat, because the journey is too great for thee." Tho it be not long, yet the way is miry; therefore obey his voice, arise and eat, "and in the strength of that meat thou mayest go to the mount of God"; and, like Moses, "die in the mount whither thou goest up"; and say, as Simeon, "Lord, now lettest thou thy servant depart in peace, for mine eye" of faith, "hath seen thy salvation."

Secondly. Concerning the fittest place for heavenly contemplation, it is sufficient to say that the most convenient is some private retirement. Our spirits need every help, and to be freed from every hindrance in the work. If, in private prayer, Christ directs us to "enter into our closet and shut the door, that our Father may see us in secret," so should we do this in meditation. How often did Christ himself retire to some mountain, or wilderness, or other solitary place! I give not this advice for occasional meditation, but for that which is set and solemn. Therefore withdraw thyself from all society, even that of godly men, that thou mayest awhile enjoy the society of thy Lord. If a student can not study in a crowd, who exerciseth only his invention and memory, much less shouldst thou be in a crowd, who art to exercise all the powers of thy soul, and upon an object so far above nature. We are fled so far from superstitious solitude that we have even cast off the solitude of contemplative devotion. We seldom read of God's appearing by himself, or by his angels, to any of his prophets or saints in a crowd; but frequently when they were alone.

But observe for thyself what place best agrees with thy spirit, within doors or without. Isaac's example, in "going out to meditate in the field," will, I am persuaded, best suit with most. Our Lord so much used a solitary garden that even Judas, when he came to betray him, knew where to find him: and tho he took his disciples thither with him, yet he "was withdrawn from them" for more secret devotions; and tho his meditation be not directly named, but only his praying, yet it is very clearly implied; for his soul is first made sorrowful with bitter meditations on his sufferings and death, and then he poureth it out in prayer. So that Christ had his accustomed place, and consequently accustomed duty; and so must we: he hath a place that is solitary, whither he retireth, even from his own disciples; and so must we: his meditations go further than his thoughts; they affect and pierce his heart and soul, and so must ours. Only there is a wide difference in the object: Christ meditates on the sufferings that our sins had deserved, so that the wrath of his Father passed through all his soul; but we are to meditate on the glory he hath purchased, that the love of the Father and the joy of the Spirit may enter our thoughts, and revive our affections, and overflow our souls.

Thirdly. I am next to advise thee concerning the preparation of thy heart for this heavenly contemplation. The success of the work much depends on the frame of thy heart. When man's heart had nothing in it to grieve the Spirit, it was then the delightful habitation of his Maker. God did not quit his residence there till man expelled him by unworthy provocations. There was no shyness or reserve till the heart grew sinful and too loathsome a dungeon for God to delight in. And were this soul reduced to its former innocency, God would quickly return to his former habitation, yea, so far as it is renewed and repaired by the Spirit, and purged from its lusts, and beautified with his image, the Lord will yet acknowledge it as his own: Christ will manifest himself unto it, and the Spirit will take it for his temple and residence. So far as the heart is qualified for conversing with God, so far it usually enjoys him. Therefore, "with all diligence keep thy heart, for out of it are the issues of life." More particularly,

1. Get thy heart as clear from the world as thou canst. Wholly lay by the thoughts of thy business, troubles, enjoyments, and every thing that may take up any room in thy soul. Get it as empty as thou possibly canst, that it may be the more capable of being filled with God. If thou couldst perform some out-

ward duty with a part of thy heart while the remainder is absent, yet this duty, above all, I am sure thou canst not. When thou shalt go into the mount of contemplation, thou wilt be like the covetous man at the heap of gold, who, when he might take as much as he could, lamented that he was able to carry no more: thou wilt find as much of God and glory as thy narrow heart is able to contain, and almost nothing to hinder thy full possession but the incapacity of thy own spirit. Then thou wilt think, "O that this understanding and these affections could contain more! It is more my unfitness than any thing else that even this place is not my heaven. 'God is in this place, and I knew it not.' This 'mount is full of chariots of fire'; but mine eyes are shut, and I can not see them. O the words of love Christ hath to speak, and wonders of love he hath to show, but I can not bear them yet! Heaven is ready for me, but my heart is unready for heaven." Therefore, reader, seeing thy enjoyment of God in this contemplation much depends on the capacity and disposition of thy heart, seek him here, if ever, with all thy soul. Thrust not Christ into the stable and the manger, as if thou hadst better guests for the chief rooms. Say to all thy worldly business and thoughts, as Christ to his disciples, "Sit ye here, while I go and pray yonder"; or as Abraham to his servants, when he went to offer Isaac, "Abide ye here, and I will go yonder and worship, and come again to you." Even as "the priests thrust king Uzziah out of the temple," where he presumed to burn incense, when they saw the leprosy upon him; so do thou thrust those thoughts from the temple of thy heart, which have the badge of God's prohibition upon them.

2. Be sure to enter upon this work with the greatest solemnity of heart and mind. There is no trifling in holy things. "God will be sanctified in them that come nigh him." These spiritual, excellent, soul-raising duties are, if well used, most profitable; but, when used unfaithfully, most dangerous. Labor, therefore, to have the deepest apprehensions of the presence of God and his incomprehensible greatness. If Queen Esther must not draw near "till the king hold out the sceptre," think, then, with what reverence thou shouldst approach him who made the worlds with the word of his mouth, who upholds the earth as in the palm of his hand, who keeps the sun, moon and stars in their courses, and who sets bounds to the raging sea! Thou art going to converse with him before whom the earth will quake and devils do tremble, and at whose bar thou and all the world must shortly stand

and be finally judged. O think! "I shall
then have lively apprehensions of his majesty.
My drowsy spirits will then be awakened, and
my irreverence be laid aside: and why should
I not now be roused with the sense of his
greatness, and the dread of his name possess
my soul?" Labor also to apprehend the
greatness of the work which thou attemptest,
and to be deeply sensible both of its importance and excellency. If thou wast pleading
for thy life at the bar of an earthly judge,
thou wouldst be serious, and yet that would
be a trifle to this. If thou wast engaged in
such a work as David against Goliath, on
which the welfare of a kingdom depended, in
itself considered, it were nothing to this.
Suppose thou wast going to such a wrestling
as Jacob's, or to see the sight which the three
disciples saw in the mount, how seriously,
how reverently wouldst thou both approach
and behold! If but an angel from heaven
should appoint to meet thee at the same time
and place of thy contemplations, with what
dread wouldst thou be filled! Consider, then,
with what a spirit thou shouldst meet the
Lord, and with what seriousness and awe thou
shouldst daily converse with him. Consider,
also, the blessed issue of the work, if it succeed; it will be thy admission into the presence
of God, and the beginning of thy eternal glory

on earth; a means to make thee live above
the rate of other men, and fix thee in the
next room to the angels themselves, that thou
mayest both live and die joyfully. The prize
being so great, thy preparations should be
answerable. None on earth live such a life
of joy and blessedness as those who are acquainted with this heavenly conversation.
The joys of all other men are but like a child's
plaything, a fool's laughter, or a sick man's
dream of health. He that trades for heaven
is the only gainer, and he that neglects it
is the only loser. How seriously, therefore,
should this work be done!

A Prayer of Thomas Arnold

O gracious Father, keep me through thy
holy Spirit; keep my heart soft and tender
now in health and amidst the bustle of the
world; keep the thought of thyself present to
me as my Father in Jesus Christ; and keep
alive in me a spirit of love and meekness to
all men, that I may be at once gentle and
active and firm. O strengthen me to bear
pain, or sickness, or danger, or whatever thou
shalt be pleased to lay upon me, as Christ's

soldier and servant; and let my faith overcome the world daily. Perfect and bless the work of thy Spirit in the hearts of all thy people, and may thy kingdom come, and thy will be done in earth as it is in heaven. I pray for this, and for all that thou seest me to need, for Jesus Christ's sake. AMEN.

A Discourse Treating of Legal Righteousness, of Evangelical Righteousness, or the Righteousness of Faith

BY

JOHN SMITH

JOHN SMITH

One of the founders of the "Cambridge Platonists," was born at Achurch, Northamptonshire, England, in 1618, and died August 7, 1652. He studied at Emmanuel College, Cambridge (B. A., 1640; M. A., 1644, in which year he was chosen fellow of Queen's). At Queens he labored as Hebrew lecturer, censor philosophicus, Greek praelector, and became dean of the college and catechist, in 1650. He seems to have shown something of Whichcote's marvelous power as a teacher, and to have been of pure and lofty character. His "Select Discourses," published in 1660, 1673, 1821, and (Cambridge Press) 1859, is practically all he left behind him. These "Discourses" are animated by the breath of a high, divine reason, and show a logic almost as keen and direct as Chillingworth's, and an imagination as rich as Jeremy Taylor's.

How the Gospel Righteousness Is Conveighed to Us By Faith, Made to Appear from These Two Considerations

[In this selection the original spelling has been retained.]

We come now to shew the way by which God-like and gospel-righteousness is conveighed to us; and that is by faith. This is that powerful attraction which by a strong and divine sympathy draws down the vertue of heaven into the souls of men, which strongly and forcibly moves the souls of good men into a conjunction with that divine goodness by which it lives and grows: This is that divine impress that invincibly draws and sucks them in by degrees into the Divinity, and so unites them more and more to the centre of life and love: it is something in the hearts of men which, feeling by an occult and inward sensation the mighty insinuations of the divine goodness, immediately complies with it, and with the greatest ardency that may be is perpetually rising up into conjunction with it; and being first begotten and enlivened by the warm beams of that goodness, it alwaies breaths and gasps after it for its constant growth and nourishment. It is then fullest of life and vivacity when it partakes most freely of it; and perpetually languisheth when it is in any measure deprived of that sweet and pure nourishment it derives from it.

But that we may the more clearly unfold this business, How gospel-righteousness comes to be communicated through faith, we shall lay it forth in two particulars.

First, the gospel lays a strong foundation of a chearfull dependance upon the grace and love of God, and affiance in it. We have the greatest security and assurance that may be given us of God's readiness to relieve such forlorn and desolate creatures as we are: That there are no such dreadful fates in heaven as are continually thirsting after the bloud of sinners, insatiably greedy after their prey, never satisfied till they have devoured the souls of men. Lest we should by such dreadful apprehensions be driven from God, we are told of the bloud of sprinkling that speaks better things for us; of a mighty Favourite solliciting our cause with perpetual intercessions in the court of heaven; of a new and living way to the throne of grace and to the holy of holies which our Saviour hath consecrated through his flesh. We are told of a great and mighty Saviour able to save to the utmost all that come to God by him: we hear of the most compassionate and tender promises

that may be from the truth itself, that who-
soever comes to him he will in no wise cast
out; that they that believe on him, out of them
should flow streams of living water. We
hear of the most gracious invitations that
heaven can make to all weary and heavy-
laden sinners to come to Christ, that they may
find rest: the great secrets of heaven and the
arcana of divine counsells are revealed, whereby we are acquainted that glory to God in the
highest, peace on earth, good will towards
men, are sweetly joyned together in heaven's
harmony, and happily combin'd together in
the composure of it's ditties: That the glory
of the Deity and salvation and men are not
allaied by their union one with another, but
both exalted together in the most transcendent
way, that divine love and bounty are the su-
pream rulers in heaven and earth. There is
no such thing as sowre despight and envy
lodged in the bosome of that ever-blessed
Being above, whose name is Love, and all
whose dispensations to the sons of men are
but the dispreadings and distended radiations
of his love, as freely flowing forth from it
through the whole orbe and sphear of its
creation as the bright light from the sun in
the firmament, of whose benign influences we
are then onely deprived when we hide and
withdraw our selves from them. We are

taught that the mild and gentle breathings of the divine spirit are moving up and down in the world to produce life, and to revive and quicken the souls of men into a feeling sense of a blessed immortality. This is that mighty spirit that will, if we comply with it, teach us all things, even the hidden things of God; mortifie all the lusts of rebellious flesh, and seal us up to the day of redemption. We are taught that with all holy boldness we may in all places lift up holy hands to God, without wrath or doubting, without any sowre thoughts of God, or fretfull jealousies, or harsh surmises. We can never distrust enough in our selves, nor ever trust too much in God. This is the great plerophory, and that full confidence which the gospel every where seems to promote: and should I run through all the arguments and solicitations that are there laid down, to provoke us to an entertainment hereof, I should then run quite through it from one end to another: it containing almost nothing else in the whole complex and body of it but strong and forcible motives to all ingenuous addresses to God, and the most effectual encouragement that may be to all chearfull dependance on him, and confident expectation of all assistance from him to carry on our poor endeavours to the atchievment of blessedness, and that in the most plain and simple

way that may be without any double mind or
mental reservation; heaven is not acquainted
so feelingly with our wicked arts and devices.
But it is very strange that where God writes
life so plainly in fair capital letters, we are
so often apt to read death; that when he tells
us over and over, that hell and destruction
arise from our selves, that they are the workmanship of our own hands, we will needs
understand their pedigree to be from heaven,
and that they were conceived in the womb of
life and blessedness. No, but the gospel tells
us we are not come to mounts of burning, nor
unto blackness and darkness and tempest, etc.
(Heb. 12:18). Certainly a lively faith in
this love of God, and a sober converse with
his goodness by a cordial entertainment and
through perswasion of it, would warm and
chafe our benumbed minds, and thaw our
hearts frozen with self-love; it would make us
melt and dissolve out of all self-consistency,
and by a free and noble sympathy with the
divine love to yield up our selves to it, and
dilate and spread our selves more fully in it.
This would banish away all atheisme and ire-
full slavish superstition; it would cast down
every high thought and proud imagination
that swells within us and exalts it self against
this soveraign deity; it would free us from
all those poor, sorry, pinching, and particular

loves that here enthrall the souls of men to
vanity and baseness; it would lead us into the
true liberty of the sons of God, filling our
hearts once enlarged with the sense of it with
a more generous and universal love, as un-
limited and unbounded as true goodness it
self is. Thus Moses-like conversing with God
in the Mount, and there beholding his glory
shining thus out upon us in the face of Christ,
we should be deriving a copy of that eternal
beauty upon our own souls, and our thirst
and hungry spirits would be perpetually sucking in a true participation and image of his
glory. A true divine love would wing our
souls, and make them take their flight swiftly
towards heaven and immortality. Could we
once be thoroughly possess'd and mastered
with a full confidence of the divine love, and
God's readiness to assist such feeble, languish-
ing creatures as we are, in our assays after
heaven and blessedness, we should then, finding our selves born up by an eternal and almighty strength, dare to adventure courage-
ously and confidently upon the highest de-
signes of happiness, to assail the kingdom of
heaven with a holy gallantry and violence, to
pursue a course of well-doing without weariness; knowing that our labour shall not be in
vain in the Lord, and that we shall receive
our reward, if we faint not: we should work

out our salvation in the most industrious manner, trusting in God as one ready to instill strength and power into all the vital faculties of our souls: we should press towards the mark, for the prize of the high calling of God in Christ Jesus, that we may apprehend that for which also we are apprehended of Christ Jesus. If we suffer not our selves to be robb'd of this confidence and hope in God as ready to accomplish the desires of those that seek after him, we may then walk on strongly in the way to heaven and not be weary; we may run and not faint. And the more the souls of men grow in this blissful perswasion, the more they shall mount up like eagles into a clear heaven, finding themselves rising higher and higher above all those filthy mists, those clouds and tempests of a slavish fear, despair, fretfulness against God, pale jealousies, wrathfull and embittered thoughts of him, or any strugglings or contests to get from within the verge of his power and omnisciency, which would mantle up their souls in black and horrid night.

I mean not all this while by this holy boldness and confidence and presence of mind in a believer's converse with the deity, that high pitch of assurance that wafts the souls of good men over the Stygian lake of death, and brings them to the borders of life; that here puts them into an actual possession of bliss, and reestates and reestablishes them in paradise; No, that more general acquaintance which we may have with God's philanthropy and bounty, ready to relieve with the bowells of his tender compassions all those starving souls that call upon him (for surely he will never doe less for fainting and drooping souls than he doth for the young ravens that cry unto him); that converse which we are provoked by the gospel to maintain with God's unconfined love, if we understand it aright, will awaken us out of our drawsie lethargy, and make us ask of him the way to Sion with our faces thitherward. This will be digging up fresh fountains for us while we goe through the valley of Baca, whereby refreshing our weary souls we shall goe on from strength to strength until we see the face of our loving, and ever-to-be-loved, God in Sion. And so I come to the next particular wherein we shall further unfold how this God-like righteousness, we have spoken of, is conveighed to us by faith: and that is this.

2. A true gospel-faith is no lazy or languid thing, but a strong ardent breathing for and thirsting after divine grace and righteousness; it doth not onely pursue an ambitious project of raising the soul immaturely to the condition of a darling favourite with heaven, while it

is unripe for it, by procuring a meer empty
pardon of sin; it desires not onely to stand
upon clear terms with heaven by procuring
the crossing of all the debt-books of our sins
there; but it rather pursues after an internal
participation of the divine nature. We often
hear of a saving faith; and that, where it is,
is not content to wait for salvation till the
world to come; it is not patient of being an
expectant in a probationership for it until
this earthly body resignes up all its worldly
interest, that so the soul might then come
into its room. No, but it is here perpetually
gasping after it, and effecting of it in a way
of serious mortification and self-denial: it enlarges and dilates itself as much as may be
according to the vast dimensions of the divine love, that it may comprehend the height
and depth, the length and breadth thereof,
and fill the soul, where it is seated, with all
the fullness of God: it breeds a strong and
unsatiable appetite where it comes after true
goodness. Were I to describe it, I should
doe it no otherwise than in the language of
the apostle; it is that whereby we live in
Christ, and whereby he lives in us; or, in the
dialect of our Saviour himself, something so
powerfully sucking in the precious influences
of the divine Spirit that the soul, where it
is, is continually flowing with living waters

issuing out of itself. A truely-believing soul by an ingenuous affiance in God and an eager thirst after him is alwaies sucking from the full breasts of the divine love; thence it will not part, for there, and there onely, is its life and nourishment; it starves and faints away with grief and hunger, whensoever it is pull'd away from thence; it is perpetually hanging upon the arms of immortal goodness, for there it finds its great strength lies; and as much as may be armes itself with the mighty power of God, by which it goes forth like a giant refreshed with wine to run that race of grace and holiness that leads to the true Elysium of glory, and that heavenly Canaan which is above. And whensoever it finds itself enfeebled in its difficult conflict with those fierce and furious corruptions, those tall sons of Anak, which arising from our terrene and sensual affections doe here encounter it in the wilderness of this world; then turning itself to God, and putting itself under the conduct of the angel of his presence, it finds itself presently out of weakness to become strong, enabled from above to put to flight those mighty armies of the aliens. True faith (if you would know its rise and pedegree), it is begotten of the divine bounty and fulness manifesting itself to the spirits of men, and it is conceived and brought forth by a deep and humble sense of self-indigency and poverty. Faith arises out of self-examination, seating and placing itself in view of the divine plenitude and all-sufficiency; and thus (that I may borrow those words of St. Paul) we received the sentence of death in our selves, that we should not trust in our selves but in him. The more this sensual, brutish and self-central life thrives and prospers, the more divine faith languisheth; and the more that decays, and all self-feeling, self-love, and self-sufficiency pine away, the more is true faith fed and nourished, it grows more vigorous: and as carnal life wasts and consumes, so the more does faith suck in a true divine and spiritual life from the true Ἀυτοϛωὴ ("Self-subsistent One") who hath life in himself, and freely bestowes it to all those that heartily seek for it. When the Divinity united itself to humane nature in the person of our Saviour, he then gave mankind a pledge and earnest of what he would further doe therein, in assuming of it into as near a conjunction as might be with himself, and in dispensing and communicating himself to man in a way as far correspondent and agreeable as might be to that first copy. And therefore we are told of "Christ being formed in us" and "the Spirit of Christ dwelling in us," of our "being conformable to him, of having fellowship with him, of being as he was in this world, of living in him and his living in us, of dying, and rising again, and ascending with him into heaven,'' and the like: because indeed the same Spirit that dwelt in him derives itself in its mighty virtue and energy through all believing souls, shaping them more and more into a just resemblance and conformity to him as the first copy and pattern: whence it is that we have so many waies of unfolding the union between Christ and all believers set forth in the gospel. And all this is done for us by degrees through the efficacy of the eternal Spirit, when by a true faith we deny our selves and our own wills, submit our selves in a deep sense of our own folly and weakness to his wisdom and power, comply with his will, and by a holy affiance in him subordinate our selves to his pleasure: for these are the vital acts of a gospel-faith.

And according to this which hath been said I suppose we may fairly gloss upon St. Paul's discourses which so much prefer faith above works. We must not think in a gyant-like pride to scale the walls of heaven by our own works, and by force thereof to take the strong fort of blessedness, and wrest the crown of glory out of God's hands whether he will or no. We must not think to commence a suit in heaven for happiness upon such a poor

John Smith

and weak plea as our own external compliance
with the old law is. We must not think to
deal with God in the method of commutative
justice, and to challenge eternal life as the
just reward of our great merits, and the hire
due to us for our labour and toil we have
took in God's vineyard. No, God resists the
proud, but gives grace to the humble: it must
be an humble and self denying address of a
soul dissolved into a deep and piercing sense
of its own nothingness and unprofitableness,
that can be capable of the divine bounty: he
"fills the hungry with good things, but the
rich he sends empty away." They are the
hungry and thirsty souls, alwaies gasping
after the living springs of divine grace, as
the parched ground in the desert doth for
the dew of heaven, ready to drink them in
by a constant dependance upon God: souls
that by a living, watchfull and diligent faith
spreading forth themselves in all obsequious
reverence and love of him, wait upon him, as
the eyes of an handmaid wait on the hand of
her mistress: These are they that he delights
to satiate with the goodness. Those that being
master'd by a strong sense of their own in-
digency, their pinching and pressing poverty,
and his all-sufficient fulness, trust in him as
an almighty Saviour, and in the most ardent
manner pursue after that perfection which

his grace is leading them to; those that cannot satisfie themselves in a bare performance of some external acts of righteousness, or an external observance of a law without them, but with the most greedy and fervent ambition pursues after such an acquaintance with his divine Spirit as may breath an inward life through all the powers of their souls, and beget in them a vital form and soul of divine goodness; these are the spiritual seed of faithfull Abraham, the sons of the free-woman, and heirs of the promises, to whom all are made yea and amen in Christ Jesus. These are they which shall abide in the house for ever, when the sons of the bond-woman, those that are only Arabian proselytes, shall be cast out.

A Prayer from the Book of Hours

Almighty and everlasting God, from whom cometh every good and perfect gift, mercifully grant that the frequent meditation of thine infinite goodness may make us to love thee above all things; that we may here stedfastly believe what we do not see, and hereafter, in the blessed vision of thy glory, see what we now can not comprehend: through Jesus Christ our Lord. AMEN.

SELECTIONS FROM

Thoughts On Religion

ALSO

A Prayer

BY

BLAISE PASCAL

BLAISE PASCAL

French philosopher, mathematician, mystic, and author of great distinction; was born at Clermont Ferrand in Auvergne, June 19, 1623; died at Paris, August 19, 1662. His surroundings, as well as his natural inclinations, turned his attention early in life to scientific and mathematical problems. His attainments in mathematics are evidenced by his "Essai pour les Coniques," written before he was seventeen, and the calculating machine which he put before the public in 1642. After the death of his father in 1651, his sister Jacqueline felt free to carry out her long-cherished wish to enter Port Royal. On one of Pascal's visits to his sister there he heard a sermon that stirred him deeply, and resulted in his conversion (1653). He sought strength and protection for his new inner life in the solitude of Port Royal. There he subjected himself to the strictest discipline and took up with avidity the study of the Bible and the Church Fathers. Arnauld, "the chief light" of Port Royal, was cited before the Sorbonne for heretical doctrines. The Port Royalists, anxious to bring the question (that is, of heretical doctrine) before a wider tribunal, asked Pascal to treat it in such a way as to appeal to the popular mind. This he did in the first of the "Provincial Letters," issued without the author's name (1656). This was followed by eighteen more "Letters" (in the eleventh he came out under his own name). Tho suffering from impaired health, he stood boldly "as the champion of freedom of conscience, of truth and justice, against the all-powerful Jesuits, without fear of the Bastille or galleys." Pascal's "Pensées" (1669) are detached thoughts, and were intended as materials to be shaped into his projected "Apology for the Christian Faith."

Faith Without Reasoning

If I had but seen a miracle, say some men,
I should be converted? They would not talk
in this manner, if they knew what conversion
really meant. They imagine there is nothing
in it but merely to acknowledge there is a
God; and that to worship him consists only
in uttering certain verbal addresses, but little
different from those which the heathens made
to their idols. True conversion consists in
deep abasement of ourselves before that sovereign Being whom we have so often provoked,
and who every moment might justly destroy
us; in acknowledging that we can do nothing
without his aid, and that we have merited nothing of him but his displeasure. It consists in
knowing that there is such an invincible opposition between God and ourselves, that without a Mediator there could not be any communion between us.

Think it not strange that illiterate persons
should believe without reasoning. God gives
them the love of his righteousness, and an
hatred of themselves. He inclines their hearts
to believe. No man ever believes with a true
and saving faith unless God inclines his heart;
and no man when God does incline his heart,

can refrain from believing. This David well knew when he prayed, "Incline my heart, O God, unto thy testimonies" (Ps. 119:36).

If some men believe without having examined the proofs of religion, it is because there is produced in them a disposition truly holy; and because what they hear affirmed of our religion is perfectly agreeable to that disposition. They are sensible that God is their Maker; they are resolved to love none but him, and to hate none but themselves; they feel that they are without strength, that they are incapable of going to God, and that, unless he is pleased to come to them, they can not have any communion with him; and they hear our religion declare that we are to love God alone, and hate only ourselves; and that, whereas we are altogether corrupt and incapable of coming to God, God became man that he might unite himself to us. There needs no more than this to convince men who possess such a disposition of heart, and such knowledge of their duty and of their own incapacity to perform it.

Those whom we see become Christians without the knowledge of prophecies, or other such evidences, form as sound a judgment of their religion as those who have that knowledge. They judge of it by the heart, as others judge by the understanding. God himself inclines them to believe, and by this means they are most effectually persuaded.

I confess, that a Christian who believes without argumentative proof is not always qualified to convince an infidel who has a great deal to say for himself. But those who are acquainted with the proofs of religion can easily demonstrate that such a believer does truly receive his faith from the inspiration of God, tho he may not be able to prove it himself.

That There Is More Advantage In Believing Than In Disbelieving the Christian Religion

Unity added to infinity, does not increase it, any more than a foot-measure increases an infinite space. What is finite, vanishes before that which is infinite, and becomes nothing. Thus does our understanding before God; and our righteousness before his righteousness.

There is not so great a disproportion between unity and infinity as there is between man's righteousness and the righteousness of God.

We know that there is an infinite; but we are ignorant of its nature. For instance, we know that numbers can not be finite: there must, therefore, be an infinity in number. But we know not what it is. It can neither be equal nor unequal, because adding unity to it can not change its nature in the least. So we may certainly know there is a God, without comprehending what he is; and you ought by no means to conclude there is no God because you can not perfectly comprehend his nature.

To convince you of his existence I shall not avail myself of faith, by which we most certainly know it; nor of some other proofs of which we are in possession, because you will not receive them. I shall argue with you only upon your own principles; and I take upon me to shew, from the manner in which you reason every day concerning things of the smallest importance, how you ought to reason respecting this; and which side you ought to take in the decision of this important question concerning the existence of God. You say, then, that we are incapable of knowing whether there is a God. Now it is certain, that either there is a God, or there is not; there can be no medium. Which part then shall we choose? Reason, you will say, is not able to determine. There is an infinite chaos between us. We play, as it were, for cross or pile, at an infinite distance. For

Blaise Pascal

which will you wager? By reason you can assure yourself neither of one nor the other. By reason you can disprove neither one nor the other.

Do not then accuse those of duplicity who have already made their choice. For you can not know that they are wrong, and have made a bad one. No, you will say, but I blame them not for making this choice, but for making any; he that takes cross, and he that takes pile, are both in the wrong; the right had been not to wager at all.

Nay, but there is a necessity to wager; the thing is placed beyond your will; you are actually embarked in it, and by not laying that God is, you in effect lay that he is not. Which side then will you take? Let us balance the gain and the loss of taking the affirmative. If you gain, you gain every thing; if you lose, you lose nothing. Wager, therefore, that he is, without delay. Well I must lay, but perhaps I shall stake too much? Let us see: supposing the chance to be equal, and that you had two lives to gain, and but one to lose, you might safely lay then. And in case there were ten to win, you would certainly be imprudent not to hazard one life for ten, at a game where the chances were even. But here is an infinite number of lives of infinite happiness, to be won on an equal risk; and the stake you venture is so petty a thing, and of so short a duration, that it is ridiculous to hesitate on the occasion.

It avails nothing to say it is uncertain that you shall win, and that your risk is certain; and that the infinite distance between the certainty of what you venture and the uncertainty of what you may win makes the finite good which you expose equal to the infinite, which is uncertain: for this is not true. Every gamester stakes what is certain against what is uncertain; and yet, by venturing a finite certainty for a finite uncertainty, he does not act contrary to reason. There is not an infinite distance between the certainty of what we venture, and the uncertainty of the prize to be gained. There is, indeed, an infinite distance between the certainty of winning and the certainty of losing. But the uncertainty of winning is proportioned to the certainty of what we venture, according to the proportion of the chance of winning or losing: hence, if there be as many chances on one side as on the other, the game is even; and then the certainty of what we venture is equal to the uncertainty of the prize, so far are they from being infinitely distant; so that the argument is of infinite force, if what we stake be finite, where the chances of winning and losing are equal, and that which may be won is infinite. We have here a demonstration, and if men are capable of comprehending any truth whatever, they can not but feel the force of this.

I own and confess it; but are there not some means of seeing a little clearer into this matter? Certainly, through the medium of Scripture, and of the other proofs of religion, which are numberless.

Men, you will say, who have the hope of salvation are so far happy; but the fear of hell is a counterpoise to their happiness.

But which, I beseech you, has most cause to be afraid of hell; he that is ignorant whether there is a hell or not, and is certain of damnation if there be; or he who is certainly persuaded there is a hell, but possesses the hope of deliverance from it.

If a man who had but eight days to live should not think it wisest to consider that as somewhat more than a mere matter of chance, he must have utterly lost his understanding. And were we not enslaved by our passions, eight days and a hundred years would, in this calculation, appear the same thing.

What harm then are you likely to sustain by taking this part. You will be faithful, honest, humble, grateful, beneficent, upright, and sincere. It is true, you will not live in poisoned pleasure, in earthly glory, in sensual delights: but will you not have others more desirable? I tell you, you will gain even in this life; and that at every step you take in this path you will discover so much certainty of advantage, and so much nullity in what you hazard, that at length you will find you have betted for a sure and infinite profit, and have in effect risked nothing to obtain it.

You say, you are so made as to be incapable of believing: at least then be persuaded of your incapacity, since altho reason invites you to it, still you can not believe. Labor then to be convinced, not by augmenting the proofs of a Deity, but by diminishing the power of your passions. You would arrive at faith, but you know not the way: you would be cured of your infidelity, and you ask what are its remedies: learn them from those who were once in your condition, but are at present without any doubt. They know the path which you would find: they have recovered from the disease of which you wish to be healed. Pursue the method with which they began: imitate their external actions, if you can not, as yet, participate their inward dispositions; quit those vain amusements which have hitherto entirely employed you.

I should soon have quitted these pleasures, say you, if I had but had faith. And I say, on the other hand, you would soon have had faith, if you had quitted your pleasures. It is your part to begin. I would give you faith if I could; I am unable to do this, and, consequently, to put the truth of what you say to the test: but you may easily abandon your pleasures, and put the truth of what I say to the test.

We must not forget our own nature; we are body as well as spirit; and hence it comes to pass that the instrument by which conviction is produced is not demonstration only. How few things are there demonstrated! Demonstrations act only on the mind; but custom produces our strongest convictions; it engages the senses, and they incline the understanding, without even giving it time for thought. Who has ever demonstrated the certainty of to-morrow's light, or of our own death? And yet what is more universally believed? Custom, therefore, persuades us of it. Custom makes so many men pagans and Turks; and so many artizans, soldiers, etc. It is true that we ought not to begin with custom in our inquiries after truth; but we must have recourse to it, when once we have discovered where truth is, in order to refresh and invigorate our belief, which every passing hour inclines us to forget; for a regular train of arguments can not always be present to our minds. We want something more easy, a habit of believing, which, without violence, or art, or argument, compels our assent, and so inclines all our powers toward it that we naturally fall into it. It will not be sufficient that we are willing to believe any thing upon the force of conviction, when our senses are soliciting us to believe directly the contrary. The two parts of ourselves must always proceed in concert; the understanding, by those arguments which it is sufficient once in our lives to have understood; the senses, by habit, and by not suffering them to take a contrary bias.

A Prayer, Imploring of God the Right Use of Sickness

O Lord, whose spirit is so good and gracious in all things, and who art so merciful that not only the prosperities, but even the distresses which happen to thine elect, are the effects of thy mercy, grant me grace not to act like a heathen in the state to which thy justice has brought me; but that, like a true Christian, I may acknowledge thee for my Father and my God, in whatsoever circumstances I am placed. For the altering of my condition can no way influence thine. Thou art ever the same, tho I am subject to change: thou art no less God when thou art afflicting and punishing, than when thou art consoling and shewing compassion.

Thou gavest me health to be spent in serving thee; and I perverted it to a use altogether profane. Now thou hast sent a sickness for my correction: O suffer me not to use this likewise to provoke thee, by my impatience. I abused my health, and thou hast justly punished me for it: O keep me from abusing thy punishment. And since the corruption of my nature is such, that it renders thy favors pernicious to me; grant, O my God, that thy all-powerful grace may render thy chastisements beneficial. If my heart has been filled with the love of the world, while I was in possession of strength, destroy my vigor to promote my salvation; and either by weakness of body, or the zeal of charity, render me incapable of enjoying the world, that my delight may be only in thee.

O God, to whom I must render an exact account of all my actions at the end of my life, and at the end of the world: O God, who only sufferest the world, and all things in the world to subsist, for the trial of thine elect and for the punishment of the wicked: O God, who leavest hardened sinners in the delicious but criminal enjoyment of this world: O God, who causest our bodies to die, and at the hour of death removest the soul from all that it loved in the world: O God, who, at that last moment of my life wilt separate me from all things to which I am attached, and on which my heart has been set: O God, who wilt, at the last day, consume the heavens and the earth, and all the creatures they contain, to shew to all mankind that nothing subsists but thyself, and that nothing is worthy of love but thee, since nothing is durable but thee: O God, who wilt destroy all these vain idols, and all these fatal objects of our affections: I praise thee, O God, and I will bless thee all the days of my life, that thou hast been pleased, in thy mercy toward me, to anticipate that awful day by already destroying all things with regard to me by this state of weakness to which thou hast reduced me. I praise thee, O my God, and I will bless thee all the days of my life, that thou hast been pleased to make me incapable of enjoying the delights of health, and the pleasures of the world; and that thou hast, for my good, in a manner destroyed those deceitful idols, which thou wilt effectually annihilate, to the confusion of the wicked, in the day of thy wrath. Grant, O Lord, that I may, in future, judge myself by this destruction, which thou hast wrought in my behalf; that thou mayest not hereafter condemn me to that utter destruction which thou wilt make of my present life, and of the world. For, O Lord, as at the instant of my death I shall find myself separated from the world, stript of all things, and standing alone in thy presence, to answer to thy justice for all the movements of my heart: grant that I may consider myself, in this disease, as in a kind of death, separated from the world, stript of all the objects of my affections, placed alone in thy presence, to implore of thy mercy the conversion of my heart; and that thus I may enjoy great consolation in knowing that thou art now sending me a sort of death, for the display of thy mercy, before thou sendest me death in reality, for the display of thy justice. Grant then, O my God, that as thou hast anticipated my death, so I may anticipate the justice of thy sentence; and that I may so examine myself, before thy judgment, that I may find mercy hereafter in thy sight.

Grant, O Lord, that I may in silence adore the order of thine adorable providence, in the disposal of my life, that thy rod may comfort me; and that—having lived in the bitterness of my sins while I was in peace—I may taste the heavenly sweetness of thy grace during the salutary afflictions with which thou hast visited me. But I confess, O my God, that my heart is so hardened, so full of worldly ideas, cares, inquietudes, and attachments, that neither health, nor sickness, nor discourses, nor books, nor thy Holy Scriptures, nor thy gospel, nor thy most holy mysteries, nor alms, nor fastings, nor mortifications, nor miracles, nor the use of the sacraments, nor the sacrifice of thy body, nor all my endeavors, nor those of the whole world together, can do anything at all even to begin my conversion, except thou accompany them all with the extraordinary assistance of thy grace. I look up, therefore, O my God, unto thee, who art God Almighty, to implore a gift which all creatures together could never bestow. I should not dare to direct my cries unto thee, were there any other that could hear them. But, O my God, as the conversion of my heart, which I ask of thee, is a work exceeding all the powers of nature, I can only apply to the Almighty Author and Master of nature. To whom, O Lord, shall I cry; to whom shall I have recourse, but unto thee? Every thing that is not God is unable to fulfil my desires. It is God himself that I ask and that I seek: it is to thee alone, O my God, whom I seek; that I may obtain thyself. O Lord, open my heart; enter into this rebellious place, that my sins have possest. They hold it in subjection; do thou enter, as into the strong man's house; but first bind the strong and powerful enemy, who is the tyrant over it;

and take to thyself the treasures which are there. Lord, take my affections which the world has robbed me of; spoil thou the world of this treasure; or rather resume it to thyself, for to thee it belongs; it is a tribute I owe thee, for thine own image is stamped upon it. Thou didst form it there, O Lord, at the moment of my baptism, which was my second birth, but now it is wholly defaced; the image of the world is so strongly engraven on it, that thine own is no longer discernible. Thou alone wast able to create my soul; thou alone art able to create it anew. Thou alone couldst form in it thine image; thou alone canst reproduce it, and reimpress that defaced image; that is to say, Jesus Christ, my Savior; the express image and character of thine essence.

O my God, how happy is the heart which can love so charming an object, where the affection is so honorable, the attachment so beneficial! I feel that I can not love the world without displeasing thee, without hurting and dishonoring myself; and yet the world is still the object of my delight. O my God, how happy are the souls whose delight thou art; for they may give themselves wholly up to the love of thee, not only without scruple, but even with commendation! How firm and lasting is their happiness! Their expectation can never be defeated; because thou failest not, and neither life nor death can ever separate them from the object of their desires. The very moment which shall involve the wicked, and their idols, in one common ruin, shall unite the just to thee in one common glory; and as the one shall perish with the perishable objects to which they had given their affections, the latter shall subsist for ever in that eternal and self-existing object to whom they are so intimately joined. O how happy are those who with the perfect liberty, and yet with the invincible inclination of their will, love perfectly and freely what they are necessarily under obligation to love.

Perfect, O my God, the good desires thou hast given me. Be thou their end, as thou art their beginning. Crown thy own gifts; for thy gifts I acknowledge them to be. I acknowledge them, O my God, and so far from presuming that my prayers have that merit that should oblige thee to grant them, I most humbly confess, that having given up to the creatures this heart which thou only formedst for thyself, and not either for the world or myself, I can expect no favor but from thy mercy, since I have nothing in me that can oblige thee to it; and all the natural movements of my heart, being directed either toward creatures, or toward myself, can only be provoking to thee. I thank thee, therefore,

O my God, for the good desires thou hast inspired; and also that thou enablest me to thank thee for them.

Touch my heart with repentance for my faults; because without this inward pain, the outward evils with which thou hast afflicted my body will be a new occasion of sin. Make me rightly to understand that the pains of the body are only the punishment, and the figure together, of those of the soul: but, O Lord, make them prove likewise the remedy, by making me consider, from the pains which I feel, those which I was not sensible of in my soul, tho it was diseased and covered with sores. For, O Lord, the greatest of its maladies is this insensibility and exceeding weakness, which has taken from it all sense of its own miseries. Make me to feel them deeply, and grant that the rest of my life may be one continued penitence, to wash away the sins I have committed. O Lord, altho my past life has been free from grievous crimes, the occasions of which thou hast kept from me; it has still been exceedingly hateful to thee, from my constant negligence, my misuse of thy most holy sacraments, my contempt of thy Word and inspirations, the idleness and total unprofitableness of my actions and thoughts; and the entire waste of all that time which thou hadst given me to worship thee, that I might in all my business seek the means of doing thy pleasure, and of becoming truly penitent for my daily trespasses—which are common to the best of men, and therefore require that their whole life should be one continued repentance, without which they are in danger of falling from their righteousness.

Thus, O my God, have I always been rebellious against thee. Yea, Lord, hitherto I have been always deaf to thy inspirations; I have despised thy oracles; I have judged contrary to what thou judgest: I have contradicted those holy maxims which thou hast brought into the world from the bosom of thine eternal Father, and according to which thou wilt judge the world. Thou hast said, "Blessed are they that mourn, and wo unto those who live in consolation." And I have said, "Unhappy are they that mourn, and most happy are they who live in consolation: happy are those who enjoy a plentiful fortune, a splendid reputation, and uninterrupted health." And for what reason did I account them happy, but because all these advantages afforded them a greater opportunity of enjoying the creatures; that is, of offending thee. Yea, Lord, I confess that I esteemed health a good, not because it is a mean of serving thee by usefulness, of employing more days and nights in thy service, and of doing good to my neighbors; but because, with it, I could abandon myself with less restraint to more of the enjoyments of this life, and better relish its fatal pleasures. Grant me grace, O Lord, to rectify my reason, and conform my sentiments to thine; that I may account myself happy in affliction, and that while I am incapable of external actions, thou mayest so purify my thoughts that they may no longer contradict thy own; that thus I may find thee within myself, while my weakness incapacitates me to seek thee without. For, O Lord, thy kingdom is in the hearts of the faithful; and I shall find it in myself, if I there discover thy Spirit and thy wisdom.

But, O Lord, what shall I do to engage thee to pour down thy Spirit on this miserable clay; all that I am is odious in thy sight; nor can I find any thing in myself that can be acceptable to thee. I see nothing O Lord, but my sufferings alone, which have some resemblance to thine. Look therefore on the evils I now labor under, and on those with which I am threatened. Behold with an eye of mercy the wounds which thy hand has made. O my Savior, who lovedst thy sufferings, even in death: O God, who for no other cause becamest incarnate after the fall of man, and didst take on thee a body—but that thou mightest suffer all the punishment that our sins have deserved: O God, who so lovest bodies exercised with sufferings, that thou didst choose for thyself a body the most loaded with sufferings that ever came into the world; accept my body—not for its own sake, nor for all that it contains, for all deserves thy wrath—but on account of the sufferings it endures, which alone can be worthy of thy love. May my sufferings invite thee to visit me. But to complete the preparation for thy stay, grant, O my Savior, that if my body has this in common with thine, that it suffers for my offenses, my soul may have this likewise in common with thy soul, to be sorrowful for those offenses; and that thus I may suffer with thee and like thee, both in my body and in my soul, for the transgressions I have committed.

Grant me, O Lord, grace to join thy consolations to my sufferings, that I may suffer like a Christian. I pray not to be exempted from pain; for this is the recompense of saints: but I pray that I may not be abandoned to the pains of nature without the comforts of thy Spirit. . . . I pray not to enjoy fulness of comfort without suffering, for that is the life of glory; neither do I pray for fulness of suffering without comfort; for that is a Jewish state: but I pray, O Lord, that I may feel at once both the pains of nature for my sins, and the consolations of thy Spirit by thy grace; for that is the true state of Christianity. O, may I never feel pain without comfort! But may I feel pain and consolation together, that I may hereafter attain to feel thy comforts only, without any mixture of pain! For so, O Lord, thou didst leave the world to languish in natural sufferings without consolation, till the coming of thine only Son; but now thou consolest and sweetenest the sufferings of thy faithful servants by the grace of thine only Son, and fillest thy saints with pure felicity in the glory of thine only Son. These are the wonderful steps by which thou hast carried on thy works. Thou hast raised me from the first; O, conduct me to the second; that I may attain the third! O Lord, this mercy I earnestly implore.

Suffer me not, O Lord, to be under such an estrangement from thee as to be able to reflect on thy soul being sorrowful, even unto death, and thy body being overcome by death for my sins, without rejoicing to suffer both in my body and in my soul. For what is more shameful, and yet more usual with Christians and with myself, than that while thou didst sweat blood for the expiation of our offenses, we should live in pleasurable gratification? and that Christians, who profess to be devoted to thee, that those who by baptism have

renounced the world to become thy followers,
that those who have solemnly pledged themselves in the face of the Church to live and
die with thee, that those who profess to believe that the world persecuted and crucified
thee, that those who believe thou didst expose thyself to the wrath of God, and to the
cruelty of men, to redeem them from their
sins; that those, I say, who believe all these
truths, who consider thy body as the sacrifice
which was offered for their salvation, who
look on the pleasures and sins of the world
as the only cause of thy sufferings, and the
world itself as thy murderer, should yet seek
to gratify their bodies by those same pleasures in that same world; and that those who
could not, without shuddering, behold a man
cherishing and caressing the murderer of his
father, who had laid down his life for that
son, should live as I have done with full delight in the world, which I know to be in
fact the murderer of him, whom I own for
my Father and my God, who was delivered
for my personal salvation, and who in his own
person bore the punishment of my sins? It
was most just, O Lord, that thou shouldst
interrupt so criminal a joy as this, with which
I solaced myself in the shadow of death.

Take, therefore, from me, O Lord, that
sorrow—which the love of myself may pro-

duce in me, from my sufferings, and from the
want of the success I wished to my designs
in this world—which had no regard to thy
glory. But create in me a sorrow conformable to thy own. Let my pains in some measure appease thy wrath: let them prove the
happy occasion of my conversion and salvation. Let me not hereafter wish for health
or life, but to spend it and end it for thee,
with thee, and in thee. I pray not for health
or sickness, life or death; but that thou
wouldst dispose of my health, my sickness,
my life, and my death for thy glory, for my
own salvation, for usefulness to thy Church
and thy saints, among whom I hope by thy
grace to be numbered. Thou alone knowest
what is expedient for me; thou art the Sovereign Master; do whatsoever thou pleasest.
Give me, or take away from me, conform my
will to thine; and grant that—with an humble
and perfect submission, and in a holy confidence—I may dispose myself to receive the
orders of thine everlasting providence, and
may equally adore whatsoever proceeds from
thee.

Enable me with constant uniformity of
mind to receive all sorts of events, forasmuch
as we know not what we ought to ask, and
I can not wish for one event rather than
another without presumption, and without

making myself a judge of, and responsible
for, those consequences which thy wisdom has
been pleased to conceal from me. O Lord,
I know that I know this one thing only—that
it is good to follow thee, and that it is wicked
to offend thee. Beyond this, I know not
what is best or worst, upon the whole. I know
not which is good for me, whether health or
sickness, riches or poverty, or anything else
in this world. For this knowledge surpasses
the wisdom both of men and of angels, and
lies hidden in the secrets of thy providence,
which I adore, and will not dare to pry into.

Grant, O Lord, that being what I am I may
conform myself to thy will; and that being
sick as I now am, I may glorify thee in my
sufferings. Without these, I could not attain
to thy glory; which thou thyself, O my Savior,
didst not please to attain but by sufferings.
It was by the marks of thy sufferings that
thou wast made known again to thy disciples: and it is by the sufferings they endure
that thou also knowest who are thy disciples.
Own me then as thy disciple, in the afflictions
which I endure, in my body and in my mind,
for the sins I have committed. And as
nothing is acceptable to God unless presented
by thee, unite my will to thine, and my sufferings to those which thou hast endured.
Unite me to thyself, fill me with thyself, and

with thy Holy Spirit. Enter into my heart,
and into my soul; there to sustain my afflictions—and to continue to endure, in me, what
remains of thy passion; which thou fulfillest
in thy members, till the perfect consummation
of thy mystical body. So that, being filled
by thee, it may be no longer I who live or
suffer, but thou, O my Savior, who livest and
sufferest in me: that having thus been a small
partaker of thy sufferings, thou mayest fill
me completely with that glory which thou
hast acquired by them; and in which thou
livest, with the Father and the Holy Ghost,
for ever and ever. AMEN.

A Prayer of Samuel Osgood

Almighty God, we give thee thanks for the
mighty yearning of the human heart for the
coming of a Savior, and the constant promise
of thy word that he was to come. In our own
souls we repeat the humble sighs and panting
aspirations of ancient men and ages, and own
that our souls are in darkness and infirmity
without faith in him who comes to bring God
to man and man to God. We bless thee for
the tribute that we can pay to him from our

very sense of need and dependence, and that our own hearts can so answer from their wilderness, the cry, "Prepare ye the way of the Lord." In us the rough places are to be made smooth, the crooked straight, the mountains of pride brought low, and the valleys of despondency lifted up. O God, prepare thou the way in us now, and may we welcome anew thy holy Child. Hosanna! blessed be he who cometh in the name of the Lord. AMEN.

Prayers

BY

SIMON PATRICK, D.D.

SIMON PATRICK

Learned English divine, born at Gainsborough, Lincolnshire, September 8, 1626; died at Ely, May 31, 1707. He was educated at Gainsborough Grammar School and at Queen's College, Cambridge, where he came under the influence of John Smith, the Platonist leader. Tho not closely connected with the work of this school, he was much interested in their views, and defended them in his "Brief Account of the New Sect of Latitudinarians" (London, 1662). He was for a time a Presbyterian minister, but took orders in the Church of England in 1654. In 1671 he was made chaplain in ordinary to the king. In 1672 he was made prebendary of Westminster, dean of Peterborough in 1679, bishop of Chichester in 1689, and in 1691 was transferred to the see of Ely. He was a voluminous author, producing fifty-one works, and is best known as a commentator. His commentary on the Old Testament down to the Song of Solomon (10 vols., London, 1695-1710) was very popular for a hundred and fifty years, and was combined with the contemporary work of William Lowth on the Prophets, Richard Arnold on the Apocrypha, Daniel Whitby on all the New Testament except the Apocalypse, and Moses Lowman on that book to make a complete commentary (London, 1809; many subsequent editions). Among his many works were: "Mensa Mystica, or a Discourse Concerning the Sacrament of the Lord's Supper" (1660); "The Heart's Ease, or a Remedy against Trouble" (1660); "The Parable of the Pilgrim" (1664); "The Christian Sacrifice" (1671); "The Dignity of the Christian Priesthood" (1704). He was one of the five original founders of the Society for promoting Christian Knowledge.

A Prayer for Humility

I fall down before thee, O Lord, the King of the World, adoring and worshiping with fear and reverence thy incomprehensible majesty. As I am thy creature, I ought in all humility to approach thee; and to acknowledge, with a deep sense of my poverty, that I have nothing but what I have received from thee. If I were in innocence and perfect soundness, as thou madest us at the first, the lowliest prostrations of mind and body would become me. But when I consider that I am an offender against thy sovereign authority, I can find no posture vile enough, wherein to present myself unto thee. O the mischief that we have done ourselves by turning our backs upon thee! which makes us now not know how to behave ourselves before thee.

I admire, praise and extol thy infinite condescension to us in Christ Jesus, by whom thou hast invited, nay beseeched us, to return to thee; and declared thyself well satisfied, if our hearty sorrow for what is past be but accompanied with an unfeigned submission and dutiful behavior to thee for the time to come.

And that is the most earnest desire of my soul, O Lord, to live in such a lively sense of

my entire dependence on thy bounty, and of
my unworthiness to enjoy the least of those
blessings which it hath bestowed on me, and
of the weakness of my body, and the narrowness of my mind; that I may never be puffed
up with a vain opinion of myself, nor offer
to lift up my will above thine, nor presume
to abuse any of the good things thou allowest
me, nor despise my brethren, nor refuse any
employment to which thy providence assigns
me, much less to forget to render to thee perpetually most thankful acknowledgments and
hearty service to the utmost of my power.
But as I am nothing without thee, so I may be
nothing in mine own eyes; and daily endeavor, in the condition wherein I am or shall
hereafter be, to employ all the talents thou
hast lent me to thy glory and honor, not my
own; acknowledging when I have done all
I can that I am but an unprofitable servant,
and have done no more than was my duty
to do. Preserve in my mind, for that end, a
constant and dear remembrance of the Lord
Jesus; that I may delight to tread in the
steps of his humility, and study to be endued
abundantly with the very same Spirit that
was in him. Settle in my heart a serious
and strong sense of the glory to which Jesus
is advanced, by humbling himself even unto
the death: that I may never seek great things

to myself in this life, nor be ambitious of
praise of men, nor use any of the gifts thou
bestowest on me to the discouragement of
my neighbor, or the trouble of Christian
society: but with true modesty and lowliness
of mind I may ever seek the profit and peace
of all. Being respectful and obedient to my
superiors; courteous among my equals; con-
descending to men of low estate; and giving
all the praise back again to thee, who art able
to promote thy worshipers and obedient servants to a crown of life and immortal happiness. I rely on thy gracious promise, that
he who humbleth himself shall be exalted:
and hope, whatever my portion is here below, that thou wilt count me worthy of that
world and of the resurrection of the dead.

I am sensible, O Lord, how unable I am
to perform or attain such great things without thy aid, for which I humbly look up unto
heaven: distrusting myself, and confiding
wholly in the power of the Lord Jesus; who
is present, I believe, by his Holy Spirit to all
those who place their strength and sufficiency
in his almighty grace.

The grace of our Lord Jesus Christ be
with me now and always. AMEN.

A Prayer for Charity

I adore, O most High and Holy One who inhabitest eternity, thine infinite wisdom, power, goodness, and all the rest of thy glorious perfections. The heaven of heavens can not contain thee; much less canst thou be comprehended by the most enlarged thoughts of our shallow minds; and yet thy greatness and majesty doth not despise us thy poor creatures; but gives us leave and encourages us to come into thy presence; yea, forcibly draws us many times toward thee, and makes us attend to thy kindness in those inestimable blessings thou designest for us. O how much are we indebted to thee for this extraordinary grace and favor which comforts my heart when I am astonished at thy greatness; and emboldens me notwithstanding, because thou art great in goodness and mercy. I rejoice to think of the greatness of thy power to protect and assist me; the greatness of thy bounty to supply and relieve me; the greatness of thy wisdom to guide and govern me; and the greatness of thy fatherly compassions to bear with my weaknesses. Pardon my follies, pity my miseries, and reward my small services and sufferings for thy sake. O how amiable is this sight, which thou hast now given me of thy majesty? and there are visible tokens of thy great love to us continually before mine eyes, which are innumerable: especially those in Christ Jesus, the son of thy love. I ought to love thee with the greatest passion. I can not but say, and heartily desire; O that I could love thee according to thine excellent goodness! O that I could love thee according as thou hast loved us! But alas! I am so far from this height of devout affection to thee that I am sometime ready to sigh in much dejection of spirit; and say: O that I did but love thee so well as myself! so well as I do other things! tho thou justly expectest I should love even my neighbor as myself; from whom I never received such benefits, as I do from thee continually. I am ashamed of myself; and blush to cast mine eyes toward thee. Thy great goodness only gives my hope, that by thinking of it daily, I shall love thee with all my heart, and soul, and strength; and my neighbor as myself. I feel my soul touched with ardent desire to be more like thee in doing good. And therefore most humbly beseech thee to present thyself continually before me, and to preserve in my mind a lively sense of thy great charity in Christ Jesus: whereby I may be powerfully moved to put on bowels of mercy, to be tender-hearted, rich in good works, ready to distribute, and willing to communicate, according to the ability which thou hast given me. I desire no greater treasure than abundance of this charity; which beareth all things, believeth all things, hopeth all things, endureth all things; disposing me always to follow after the things which make for peace, and things wherewith I may edify others. Inspire me more and more with this excellent spirit, which never faileth: but after it hath made me happy here, will lead me to a state of perfect love and friendship in the other world, together with Christ Jesus. Blessed be God, who hath chosen us in him, that we should be holy and without blame before him in love. Go on, good Lord, to finish what is begun; and touch my heart with such a delightful sense of thy grace to me, that my love may abound yet more and more in knowledge, and in all judgment; that I may approve things that are excellent; that I may be sincere and without offense till the day of Christ; being filled with the fruits of righteousness, which are by Jesus Christ, unto thy praise and glory. AMEN.

Simon Patrick

A Prayer for Meekness

O eternal God, who hast all perfections necessarily in thyself, and canst not but be what thou art. We are all poor things, that wholly depend on thee; having no higher perfection than to know and acknowledge thee to be the author of all good; to praise thee; to bless thee, and humbly devote ourselves to thy obedience. I see thy greatness and majesty in all thy works of wonder; I acknowledge the wisdom of thy government; the holiness and goodness of all thy laws; the riches of thy grace in thy precious promises; thy faithfulness and truth in the performance of them; and thy unwearied, long-suffering kindness in all thy entreaties and beseechings that we would be thine; and do that which we ought to be forward of ourselves to do. I can never speak good enough of thy name, which is exalted far above all praise. But the more I speak of thee, the worse I make myself; who have so little admired, esteemed, loved and imitated thee; who alone art worthy of all the honor, glory and service, that I and all creatures can render to thee. O how marvelous is thy loving-kindness, which bears with such senseless and ungrateful creatures as we are! But thy kindness is more than marvelous; having sent thy son to seek and to save us when we were lost; and with much clemency and long-suffering to attend upon us, and wait to be gracious to us, even when we are regardless of so great love. I had not been now alive, much less in the possession of such innumerable good things as both soul and body are blessed withal; if thou hadst not in much compassion passed by my folly, and still continued to spare me, and not to deal with me in thine anger and heavy displeasure. I most heartily thank thee, O Father of mercies, for this thy singular indulgence: And offer up myself to be conformed unto thee in goodness, patience, and long-suffering toward others. Hold before mine eyes continually the meekness and gentleness of Christ Jesus my Lord; that admiring the calm and quiet disposition of his spirit, I may learn of him to show all meekness unto all men.

For which end I desire to increase and grow continually in the humility and charity, of which he hath also given us so rare an example. That remembering the weakness of my own nature, and thy most tender forbearing mercy toward me, I may be the more disposed to bear with the infirmities of my neighbors; and not be easily provoked, nor behave myself unseemly: but out of a good conversation show forth my works with meek-

Simon Patrick

ness of wisdom. And since I am exposed to
such a world of temptations, excite me, O
Lord, to the greater watchfulness over my
spirit: that whatsoever sudden passion may
arise there, it may never proceed to rage and
fury, much less to brawling and reviling.
But defend me through an awful sense of thy
gracious presence with me, from grieving thy
Holy Spirit, by any bitterness or wrath, or
anger, or clamor, or evil speaking, and malice.
And fill me so with all the fruits of the
Spirit, with love, joy peace, long-suffering,
gentleness, goodness, temperance and faith,
that I may be an honor to my religion: and
find rest to my soul at present, and at last
enter into the eternal rest and refreshment
prepared for thy people, through Christ
Jesus. AMEN.

A Prayer for Patience

O Father of Mercies, and God of all comforts; who to all thy other benefits wherewith
thou continually loadest us, hast bestowed
upon us the gospel of thy grace: that we
through patience and comfort of the holy
Scriptures might have hope: accept of the
humble and thankful acknowledgments which
I make to thy divine goodness, for this riches
of mercy in Christ Jesus: who was pleased

for our sake to humble himself to death, even the death of the cross; and with great patience to suffer the sharpest pains and agonies, with many reproaches and contradictions of sinners. And when he was opprest, and afflicted, and blasphemed, yet silently endured: being brought as a lamb to the slaughter, and as a sheep before the shearer is dumb, so opened he not his mouth. I praise and magnify with all my soul his wonderful love to us, and his perfect subjection to thee: beseeching thee to fix in my heart such an ardent love to his blessed memory, and such an high admiration of his glorious example, that I may be inspired thereby with Christian resolution to follow after him in all the paths of humble, meek, and patient virtue. O that I may feel myself prest by the mighty power of that love, not only to be a doer of thy will, but for conscience toward thee, my God, to endure grief, suffering wrongfully; and to run with patience the whole race that is set before us: looking unto Jesus, the author and finisher of our faith, who for the joy that was set before him, endured the cross, despising the shame, and is set down at the right hand of the throne of God. Preserve in me such a reverence toward thee, the Father of Spirits, that I may neither despise nor faint under thy corrections: But tho thou bringest me into great and sore troubles, I may still be in subjection to thee, and live in hope of that immortal glory. And not only so, but I may rejoice, and glory also in tribulations for Christ's sake, knowing that tribulation worketh patience; and patience, experience; and experience, hope; and hope maketh not ashamed.

And whatsoever the cross be, which lies in my way to heaven, O that I may never turn aside, in the least, from thee to avoid it: but take it up willingly, and bear it as long as thou pleasest; without murmuring or repining, and with some courage and cheerfulness of spirit. And as for the common miseries of this life, endue my spirit with such principles of wisdom, and help me to preserve it in such innocence, clearness and integrity, that it may be able to sustain my infirmity; and whatsoever sicknesses, or pains, or other bodily calamities befall me, I may receive them and bear them with an equal and constant mind: knowing that as we receive good from thy hand, we ought in reason to receive evil; and in every thing to give thanks, which is thy will concerning us in Christ Jesus.

O blessed Lord, lead me whither thou pleasest, I will follow thee without complaint. I submit to thy orders: I reverence thy wisdom: I trust myself with thy goodness; I depend upon thy almighty power; I rely on thy promises; beseeching thee to support me, till patience having its perfect working in me, I may be perfect, and entire, wanting nothing. I know the time is but short, and that thou hast prepared long joys to recompense our momentary sorrows; help me therefore always to possess my soul in patience at present (giving thanks for the hope we have as an anchor of the soul both sure and stedfast) that so I may at last, after I have done thy will, O God, inherit the promise. AMEN.

For Love to This Holy Communion

O blessed Lord, who to all other acts of grace and mercy, which surpasses all our thoughts, hast been pleased to add this great kindness of instituting and ordaining holy mysteries, as pledges of thy love, and for a continual remembrance of thy death and passion, till thy glorious appearing: I praise and magnify thy wondrous goodness; I acknowledge the wisdom of thy love; I thank thee for thy most tender care of our salvation, and rejoice in the power of majesty which thou hast at the right hand of the Father, as the reward of thy humble obedience unto the death. I resolve, O Lord of life and glory, to follow thee in that obedience; and here submit myself again most willingly to all thy holy commands; beseeching thee to inspire me with such a love to every one of them that I may cleave unto them as my life and happiness. And since I have felt so often the power of thy love at that holy feast which thou hast appointed, uniting my heart unto thee, exciting by obedience, and filling me with hope and heavenly joy in thee: O that I may be strongly inclined to do this for ever in honor of thee, and thankful remembrance of thy exceeding great charity in laying down thy life for us. Thou hast said, Ye are my friends, if ye do whatsoever I command you. My heart saith unto thee, Whatsoever thou commandest, Lord, I will do. Only dispose me, I beseech thee, to delight to do thy will, O Lord: and especially to commemorate thy dying love with the most cheerful devotion of a grateful heart. I am ashamed to remember such a friend with cold, and dull, and restless affections; and therefore most earnestly desire thee always to represent thy loving-kindness so lively to me, that I may feel my spirit moved to such hearty acknowledgments of it as may make me offer up continually my soul and body, with the most ardent love to thy service. May it please thee to possess my mind with such a constant sense of my deep obligations to

thee; that I may gladly receive all occasions
to shew forth thy praise, and profess myself
thy servant, and renew my vows, and give thee
thanks for all thy benefits, and glory in the
assured hope I have of thy grace and mercy
to eternal life. And O that the rest of my
time in this world may pass away in purity,
righteousness, charity and godliness; and that
I may make a great increase in these and all
other Christian virtues, by every new remembrance of thee; till I have perfected holiness
in thy fear. That so I may feel myself to be
thy friend; and rejoice more and more in an
humble confidence that thou wilt never leave
me nor forsake me: but in the end conduct
me to feast with thee in the joys of everlasting
love. AMEN.

A Prayer for Faith In God

O eternal God; the sovereign of the world;
the perfection of beauty, the full and satisfying good, the joy of all those that know thee
and have hope in thee; who art always the
same, and canst be nothing but what thou
art, the infinitely wise, just and gracious: I
cast down myself before thee in an humble
sense, that I am beyond all expression be-
holden to thee. I received my very being from
thee, with all the comforts belonging to it;

and thou hast maintained and protected me
in the enjoyment of them many years, even
when I little thought of thy infinite bounty.
Thou hast borne with my follies with great
patience; and not only expected but invited
and beseeched my return to the obedience I
owe thee. O how marvelous is thy love in
Christ Jesus, whom thou hast sent on this
message to wretched sinners? How many
tokens and pledges have I received of thy
grace? and what treasures of joy do I find
laid up in thy great and precious promises?
I can do no less than make an oblation of
myself, with an heart full of love and thankfulness to thee for the benefits thou hast already bestowed on me, and possest with an
entire trust and confidence in thee, for what
thou shalt see good for me hereafter. I doubt
not, O Lord, of thy merciful care and providence over me, of whose tender love I have
had so great and long experience. I depend
upon thy word on which thou hast caused
me to hope; that thou wilt never leave me nor
forsake me, but all things shall work together
for good to those that love thee. I stay myself upon thy almighty power, without which
nothing can come to pass; and commit myself
to thy unerring wisdom, which disposes all
things with the most excellent reason; and
by the crossest ways can conduct me to hap-

piness. I put myself wholly into thy hands;
with an humble faith in thy infinite mercies,
trusting thee both with soul and body for
ever. I wait on thee for thy gracious assistance to enable me faithfully to discharge
my duty in every condition of life; that so
when I leave the world, I may be able to commend my spirit into thy hands, as my Savior
did, hoping for a blessed resurrection of my
body, and that my soul shall enter into rest
and peace, and at last receive a crown of life.
O that I may feel the power of this faith
sweetly composing and quieting my spirit in
all events; that I may never be afraid of evil
tidings; that my heart may be fixt trusting in
thee. O Lord, dispel all inordinate cares and
solicitude of mind for the things of this life:
and settle in me such a firm persuasion that
thou art a sun and a shield, and wilt give
grace and glory, and withhold no good thing
from them that walk uprightly, that my soul
may dwell at ease, and I may never be distracted nor confused in my thoughts: but do
my duty toward thee, with evenness, and constancy, and cheerfulness of heart. Preserve
me, O Lord, that I may never trust in robbery,
or any unjust and unlawful courses; nor, if
riches increase, ever set my heart upon them.
Bear me up by thy almighty love; that in the
worst of times, I may rest in thee, and wait

patiently for thee, and never fret myself in
any wise to do evil. Thou hast been my help,
therefore I will still make thee my refuge,
and in the shadow of thy wings will I rejoice.
My soul waiteth for the Lord; he is my help
and my shield. My heart shall rejoice in him:
because I have trusted in his holy name. Let
thy mercy, O Lord, be upon me according as
I hope in thee. And keep me in perfect peace,
whose mind is stayed on thee: because I have
trusted in thee. AMEN.

A Prayer for Resignation to God's Will, and Perfect Contentment of Mind

O Lord, the Almighty Creator of the world,
the most wise Governor of all things which
thou hast made, and our most gracious and
loving Father in the Lord Jesus; by whom
thou hast abundantly declared thy good-will
to sinners, being desirous not only to receive
them again into thy favor, but to bestow
greater blessing on them than they could have
challenged from thee, if they had remained in
innocence, and never offended thee. Thou designest us to no less happiness than eternal
life; and hast laid the strongest obligations
on us to mind our own welfare, having made
our happiness so sure that if we love ourselves, and will attend at all to our own good

and satisfaction, we can not be miserable. I acknowledge, O Lord, with all thankfulness this thy tender mercy, in ordering all things so by thy Son Jesus, that we can not without the greatest negligence and inconsideration, and without a manifest force and contradiction to our own understanding, ruin and undo our immortal souls. How much do I owe thee that thou hast been pleased to call me to the knowledge of thy grace; that thou hast invited me by such precious promises; drawn me so often and so powerfully by the motions of thy Holy Spirit; and marvelously disposed and provoked me by many happy providences, only to do myself good, and seek my own eternal felicity. I see, O Lord, the strangeness and unusualness of thy love: and am ashamed of my own backwardness and untowardness of spirit; that after all this I have so little mind to be happy, and am no more serious about that which so infinitely concerns me, and by thy grace is made so easy to me. Be still so gracious, I most humbly beseech thee, as to touch my heart with such a lively sense of thy wonderful goodness, as may perfectly subdue me to thy love and obedience; and make me absolutely surrender both soul and body to thee, of whose care and kindness I am so abundantly assured. O that I may know more feelingly what a

satisfaction it is to be blessed of the Lord,
which made heaven and earth; to wait for thy
salvation in Christ Jesus; to have thy Holy
Spirit for my guide and comforter; to be
secure of thy good providence here, and to
live in hope of immortal glory hereafter.
Strengthen me with might by thy Spirit in
the inner man, that I may be able to comprehend what is the breadth, and length, and
depth, and height, and to know the love of
Christ which passeth knowledge, till I be filled
with all the fulness of thee, my God. That
being full of divine wisdom and knowledge,
full of faith, and love, and hope, and all the
fruits of righteousness, there may be no room
for any trouble or disquiet in my heart: but
with an equal mind and resigned will I may
pass through all the changes and chances of
this mortal life. I have frequently offered
up and devoted myself unto thee; and here
again I renew the surrender, delivering up
soul and body entirely to do and suffer thy
holy will and pleasure. O preserve in my
mind such an high esteem of thy infinite wisdom and goodness that I may ever cheerfully
commit myself and all I have into thy hands,
to be disposed of as thou judgest most meet
and convenient. And whatsoever thou art
pleased to order for my portion, Lord, help
me to be perfectly contented and well pleased

with it, believing it to be the result of thine
infinite understanding, and of thy fatherly
care and tender mercy; and looking at those
unseen enjoyments to which thou knowest best
by what ways to conduct and lead me, all the
time of my sojourning here in this world.
Lift up my thoughts still higher and higher
toward that holy place where the Lord Jesus
is enthroned. Fix my mind stedfastly on
that bliss, which he is gone to prepare for us;
that I may feel it drawing my heart after him
to follow his great example; and not only
satisfying me in all conditions of life, but
filling me with joy in believing, with joy unspeakable and full of glory. Unto thee, O Lord
Jesus, I commend myself. I trust thee with
my health, my estate, my friends, and all I
have. Allot what thou pleasest for us. Let
it be unto us according to thy will. Not our
will, but thy will be done. AMEN.

A Prayer for Absolute Obedience to God

O most blessed God, the Fountain of all
being and happiness; who canst as well not
be, as not be the most excellent. The highest
of our thoughts and conceptions fall infinitely
below the greatness of thy perfections: But
that little which we know of thee is the great-

est satisfaction of our mind and understanding; and when we choose thee, our wills are satisfied; and we can not will any thing else but always to make this choice, to be governed by thy counsel, to be ruled by thy will, and to commit ourselves to thy omnipotent goodness. When we fear thee, and love thee, and trust ourselves with thee, and entirely depend upon thee, and rejoice in thy mercies; all our affections are contented, and there is no trouble nor disquiet in our heart. All that we are is happy in thee: Our bodies are better, as well as our spirits, when we cheerfully obey thee. Yea, the crosses and afflictions of this life turn to our profit, by the union of our wills with thine, and our stedfast adherence to thee. There is nothing that we can wish for more, than that we may always continue as our blessed Lord and Master did, in a constant love and absolute obedience to thee in all things. For thy will is the perfect rule of righteousness, being guided by the greatest reason and judgment; and the whole world declares it to be so ready to do good, that we can not suspect the goodness of any of thy commands. We must needs confess whatsoever befall us, that thy service is perfect freedom; and the labors of religion are the greatest pleasures; and our denial of ourselves for thy sake is our gain and advantage; and our doing good to others, is doing ourselves good; and our absolute resignation to thee is the ease, the peace, and the rest of our spirits. I hope, O Lord, that having so much reason to cleave unto thee, I shall never be so miserable as to forsake thee: but that my own sense and feeling, my frequent professions and protestations, my holy vows and resolutions, all the experience I have had of thy goodness, and the many repeated tokens and pledges of thy grace and favor, will forever tie me to thee, and make me wholly thine. Pour down upon me a more abundant portion of thy Holy Spirit, that may make my thoughts more fixt upon heavenly things, my intentions more single and pure, my desires fewer and more reasonable, my hopes more spiritual and divine, the rest of my passions more subject and useful to me, and my whole conversation here in this world more sober, righteous and godly; such as becomes one who hath such excellent precepts, such precious promises, such noble hopes, and seeks, by patient continuance in well-doing, for glory, honor and immortality. Endue me with such honesty and uprightness of heart, and with such resolution and constancy of spirit, that no temptation I meet withal in this life may prevail with me to start aside from thy holy commands. For which end possess me with a lively sense of better things; that I may not judge it necessary to my happiness to be rich, or great, or honorable, or enjoy all the pleasures and delights of the flesh: but I may feel myself so happy in the knowledge and love of thee, in likeness to thee, and full expectation of that blessed state to which thy almighty goodness can prefer me, and thou hast promised, who art the Faithful and True, one day to dignify thy servants withal; that life itself may not be so dear unto me as the doing of thy will revealed in Christ Jesus. I see the glory to which he is advanced by taking upon him the form of a servant. and becoming obedient unto death, even the death of the cross. And I most heartily thank thee for making me partaker of the heavenly calling, to follow after him and tread in his steps: beseeching thee to enable me to walk worthy of thee who hast called me to thy kingdom and glory, considering the apostle and high-priest of our profession Christ Jesus, who was faithful to thee that appointedst him over thy house and family. That, doing my duty impartially toward thee and toward all men, I may at last hear that comfortable voice, Well done, good and faithful servant; enter thou into the joy of thy Lord. AMEN.

A Prayer for a Heart to Forgive Our Enemies

O Eternal God, in whom we live, and move, and have our being; and from whose bounty we receive continually innumerable blessings, the smallest of which we are unworthy of. All thy creatures tell us how good thou art, and call upon us to admire thee, to praise thee, to love and serve thee, with all our heart, and soul, and strength. Thou hast made abundance of them more particularly to serve us, and minister to our necessities. And they are all obedient to thy word, and keep in the order and place wherein thou hast set them. We are the only disorderly creatures who have wantonly misused that liberty thou hast given us, and set up our wills above thine who art the Lord of heaven and earth. And yet, so infinite is thy mercy, thou hast not chastised our presumption as it deserved; but in much compassion sent thy dear Son, with the declaration of greater kindness to us than ever. Herein thou hast commended thy love toward us, that while we were yet sinners, Christ died for us; and not only reconciled us when we were enemies; but purchased for us the blessing of friends, and children, and heirs of thy love. O the height of thy merciful kindness toward us! O exceeding riches of thy grace, wherein thou hast abounded toward us in Christ Jesus! I most thankfully acknowledge it; I rejoice in thy love which hath passed by so many offenses; and desire to have such a lasting remembrance of it in my heart as may bow my will to thy obedience, and constrain me to imitate thy great charity, in all the actions of love to thee, and to all men. It is the perfection of our nature to be made like unto thee, in wisdom and goodness. And therefore I most heartily profess myself a disciple of the ever blessed Jesus; and think it the greatest honor to follow him, the wisdom and love of thee, our heavenly Father: who mercifully healed one that came to apprehend him; and prayed for his murderers, and when he was reviled, reviled not again; when he suffered, did not threaten; but committed himself to him that judgeth righteously. O that I may feel the power of his love so possessing my heart that no enemies, persecutors, slanderers, revilers or injurious persons, may be ever able to conquer my love toward them. But I may still bear a kind and tender heart to the most enraged and provoking spirits: blessing those that curse me; praying for those who despitefully use me; returning courtesies for affronts and injuries; bewailing their sins, pitying their miseries, and endeavoring to overcome evil with good. Endue me with such a wise, considering, and sober spirit, that I may ever prefer the example of my Lord and Master before all the customs and fashions of this world; enduring the mockeries, the shame and the contempt which may be cast upon me, for the following his forgiveness and patience. Let nothing move me from my constant affection to his holy life; nor any power or opportunity that is put into my hand, tempt me to avenge myself, and to render evil for evil, or railing for railing: but contrariwise blessing, knowing that I am thereunto called, that I should inherit a blessing. And do thou, O God, to whom vengeance belongeth, pardon also and forgive those, by whom I suffer wrongfully. Deal not with them according to their sins, nor reward them according to their iniquities: But spare them, good Lord, spare them; and in the multitude of thy mercies pass by their offenses, and deny them not the grace of repentance. That they may at last submit unto our Savior, ceasing to do evil, and learning to do well; and we may all together be monuments of thy mercy, and great examples of Christian virtue; and after we have passed our days in peace and concord here, live together in eternal love and friendship, with our Lord Jesus; To whom be glory, both now and forever. AMEN.

Simon Patrick

A Prayer for Brotherly Kindness

O God, who art good, and who doest good;
and hast loved us, the children of men, so much
as not to think thine only begotten Son too
great a gift to bestow upon us: in whom thou
designest us the greatest happiness, having
shown us the way to the most pleasant life
here, and to eternal joys when we leave the
world: I thank thee, with all my soul, for
thy abundant grace, and particularly that we
are taught of thee our God to love one another; I rejoice in the beginnings of that
heavenly life, which I feel in my heart; and
that I have tasted any of the consolation that
is in Christ, of the comfort of love, of the fellowship of the Spirit, and have any bowels,
any mercies and commiseration of others. It
is the earnest desire of my soul that thy love
may be perfected in me; that I may know thou
dwellest in me, and I in thee, because thou
hast given me of thy Spirit. Possess me, O
Lord, with such a full sense of thy infinite
charity toward us, that it may enlarge more
and more the straitness and narrowness of my
spirit, and make room for all mankind in my
hearty affection, and I may desire, and seek,
and delight in their welfare and happiness.
And especially endue me with a most ardent
charity toward all Christian people; that I

may love them as my brethren, and as heirs together of the grace of life in Christ Jesus. And seeing thou hast been pleased to love us so freely and undeservedly, so abundantly, and with such an everlasting kindness, inspire me, I beseech thee with the like disposition, that I may love my brethren with a pure heart fervently. And the Lord make me to increase and abound in love toward them and toward all men, and to persevere and continue, notwithstanding all discouragements or ill requitals, to serve them in love; to the end my heart may be established unblameable in holiness before thee our Father, at the coming of our Lord Jesus Christ with all his saints. Blessed be thy divine goodness, which hath shown to us this most excellent way; and disposed me to like it, and love it, and walk in it. O incline my heart to covet earnestly to excel in this, to be a cheerful follower of thee, my God, and still to walk in love, as Christ also hath loved us, and given himself for us, an offering and a sacrifice to thee for a sweet smelling savor. Free me perfectly from all ill will, from envy, from self-seeking, from anger, from evil speaking, and all malice; that I may adorn the gospel of our Lord Jesus by living in peace, and as I have opportunity doing good unto all men, especially unto them who are of the household of faith. And O that all Christian people may be like minded, having the same love, being of one accord and of one mind: that nothing may be done through strife or vainglory; and there may be no schism in the body of Christ: but the members may have the same care one of another; and in lowliness of mind each may esteem others better than themselves, not looking every man on his own things, but every man also on the things of others. O that this mind may be in us all, which was also in Christ Jesus: that we may have compassion one of another, love as brethren, be pitiful, and courteous, endeavoring to keep the unity of the spirit in the bond of peace. And the God of love and peace be with us all. AMEN.

A Prayer for Courage In the Profession of Christianity

O Lord of heaven and earth, who art every where the rest and peace, the refuge and security, the strength, help and salvation of all those who repose an holy trust and confidence in thee: for nothing, not death itself, can separate them from thee. I adore thy infinite love, which hath assumed our nature to such a nearness to thy own, and raised the Lord Jesus from the dead, and given him glory at thy right hand; that all his faithful follow-

ers might rest assured of thy eternal care of
them, and that they shall never perish, but
have everlasting life. Blessed, blessed be thy
name for this glad tidings of great joy which
raises our spirits above this world, and places
them in quietness and safety amidst all the
troubles and dangers of this life. I stand infinitely indebted to thee for this revelation
thou hast made of thy good will to us in Christ
Jesus, and for the glorious example that he
hath set us: who before Pontius Pilate wit-
nessed a good confession, and sealed thy truth
with his blood, knowing that his flesh should
rest in hope, and that thou wouldst not suffer
thy Holy One to see corruption. O that I
may feel myself enlivened with the same spirit
which was in our Head, the Captain of our
Salvation, made perfect through sufferings,
being faithful to him to the very death, and
not doubting I shall receive a crown of life.
It is but reason that I should part with all
I have for him, and his righteousness; who
hath made himself so freely a sacrifice of inestimable value and efficiency for us sinners.
O that I could do that cheerfully, which I am
bound to do in duty; being strengthened with
all might according to his glorious power, unto
all patience and long-suffering with joyful-
ness; giving thanks to thee who hast made us
meet to be partakers of the inheritance of

the saints in light. It is a faithful saying, I know, that if we be dead with him, we shall also live with him: if we suffer, we shall also reign with him: if we deny him, he will also deny us. Defend me, O God, from so foul a wickedness as the thought of denying my Lord and Master, and his holy truth: but keep me by thy power through faith unto salvation; that the trial of my faith, being much more precious than of gold that perisheth, tho it be tried with fire, may be found unto praise and honor and glory at the appearing of Jesus Christ. Settle, confirm and strengthen me in the Christian faith; that a stedfast belief of thy precious promises, a lively hope in thee through the resurrection of the Lord Jesus, may not only bear me up with constancy and patience, under shame, reproaches, loss of liberty and goods; but inspire me with courage and undaunted resolution in all dangers, even in death itself. Fill and greaten my mind with such a powerful sense of those immortal joys that nothing may appear so dreadful here as to terrify me from my duty, or turn me aside from the paths of righteousness, charity, truth and piety: but suffering according to thy will, O God, I may commit the keeping of my soul to thee in well doing as unto a faithful Creator. And endue me, I beseech thee, with such a perfect love to my Lord and

Master Christ Jesus, as may cast out all base
fear of suffering. Fortify my heart with such
a zealous affection to his religion, that I may
not be terrified by any adversaries, nor afraid
of their threats, neither be troubled: but
sanctify thee, the Lord God, in my heart, not
fearing those that can kill the body, but thee
who canst destroy both soul and body in hell.

Regard, O Lord, the supplications of thy
servant, who here hath made an oblation of
himself wholly unto thee. And endue me with
Christian prudence as well as courage; that I
may be both as wise as a serpent, and as innocent as a dove; and never dishonor my religion either by rashness or by cowardice:
but with a discreet zeal cleave unto truth and
righteousness, saying boldly, The Lord is my
helper, and I will not fear what man shall do
unto me. In God have I put my trust, therefore shall I never be confounded. AMEN.

A Prayer for a Low Esteem of All Worldly Things

O eternal God, the King of Kings, and the
Lord of Lords; who madest the heaven and
the earth and all contained therein, by thy
almighty word, and before whom all nations
are as nothing, less than nothing and vanity.

How mean then and despicable should that little portion of this earth which we enjoy seem in our eyes, compared with thy love and favor who art the absolute sovereign Lord of all, and canst make thy servants as happy as thou pleasest? To that very love we owe whatsoever we have in it, and there is nothing we can hope for, but from the same bounty; which we ought therefore to admire, and praise, and love and cleave unto above all things which we receive from thence. Our daily experience teaches us the weakness and uncertainty of all our earthly possessions; and that we ourselves are strangers before thee and sojourners, as were all our fathers; our days on earth being as a shadow, and there is none abiding. All flesh is grass, and all the goodness thereof is as the flower of the field. When thou with rebukes doth correct man for iniquity, thou makest his beauty to consume away like a moth; surely every man is vanity. Thou only hast immortality. With thee is the fountain of life. And therefore, Lord, what wait I for? My hope is in thee, whose word abideth for ever; and hath made us a promise of immortal life, with thyself. O possess my heart with a full belief of thy holy word; and fix my thoughts and affections upon those eternal goods, which Christ Jesus hath already entered into the possession of.

Incline my heart unto thy testimonies, and not unto covetousness. Turn away mine eyes from beholding vanity: and quicken thou me in thy ways. The law of thy mouth, I know, is better than thousands of gold and silver. Help me therefore to seek for wisdom as for silver, and to search for her as for hid treasure: and make me always to prefer her before scepters and thrones, and esteem riches nothing in comparison of her; to love her above health and beauty, to choose to have her instead of light; for the light that comes from her never goeth out. And since thou only givest wisdom, and out of thy mouth cometh knowledge and understanding: O send her out of thy holy heavens from the throne of thy glory, that being present she may labor with me; that I may know what is pleasing unto thee. O that wisdom may enter into my heart, and knowledge become pleasant unto my soul; that discretion may preserve me, and understanding may keep me, to deliver me from the way of the evil man, and to lead me soberly in my doings. Let not the splendor of any thing in this world entice me to set my heart too much on wealth and dignities, and the praise of men, whose breath is in their nostrils; much less for any of these to displease thee, by forsaking the ways of righteousness, mercy and piety; which make us thy friends, and advance us to a kingdom. But settle in me such a high esteem of thy good will toward me, fill me with such an immovable love to thee, and fix mine eyes so strongly on the brightness of that immortal glory, which Christ hath brought to light by his gospel; that it may obscure the most glittering temptations in this world, and place me out of the reach, or out of the danger of them. O make me so wise, as not to disquiet myself in vain, heaping up riches, and not knowing who shall gather them: but to lay up treasures in heaven, being rich in faith and in good works; laying up in store for myself a good foundation against the time to come, that I may lay hold on eternal life. AMEN.

A Prayer of George Dawson

Grant unto us, almighty God, that we, communing with one another and with thee, may feel our hearts burn within us, until all pure, and just, and holy, and noble things of God and man may be to us lovely, and we may find nothing to fear but that which is hateful in thine eyes, and nothing worth seeking but that which is lovely and fair therein. Let the divine brightness and peace possess our souls, so that, fearing neither life nor death, we may look to thy loving-kindness and tender mercy to lift us above that which is low and mean within us, and at last to give the spirit within us the victory and bring us safe through death into the life everlasting. Hear us of thy mercy, through Jesus Christ our Lord. AMEN.